LET'S TALK

A Lucky Duck Book

SIMON BURNHAM

LET'S TALK

Using Personal Construct Psychology to Support Children and Young People

SAGE

Los Angeles • London • New Delhi • Singapore

First published 2008

SAGE Publications Ltd
1 Oliver's Yard
55 City Road
London EC1Y 1SP

SAGE Publications Inc.
2455 Teller Road
Thousand Oaks, California 91320

SAGE Publications India Pvt Ltd
B 1/I 1 Mohan Cooperative Industrial Area
Mathura Road, Post Bag 7
New Delhi 110 044

SAGE Publications Asia-Pacific Pte Ltd
33 Pekin Street #02-01
Far East Square
Singapore 048763

www.luckyduck.co.uk

Library of Congress Control Number 2007938887

British Library Cataloguing in Publication data
A catalogue record for this book is available from the British Library

ISBN 978-1-4129-2089-6

Typeset by C&M Digitals (P) Ltd., Chennai, India
Printed in India by Replika Press, Pvt. Ltd
Printed on paper from sustainable resources

Contents

Acknowledgements

Simon Burnham would like to thank: the last several cohorts of trainee educational psychologists at Southampton University on whom a lot of the raw materials for this book have been 'road tested'; colleagues from Portsmouth's Primary Behaviour Support Service (as was) for asking about PCP and managing to integrate what they found out into their work; Dr Bob Stratford for sometimes behaving ridiculously and for being a good sport; colleagues who took the trouble to give me feedback about earlier versions of the Let's Talk programme; and 'Billy' for pitching me out of my comfort zone.

Preface

I very much like the spirit of Burr and Butt's (1992) 'invitation' to the theory and practice of George Kelly's Personal Construct Psychology (PCP), so I'm borrowing that idea to give you a sense of what I'll be asking you to engage with if you proceed any further than this preface.

This book offers a personal perspective on PCP, from the point of view of someone who has been putting it into practice through a process of alternately wrestling with and embracing Kelly's ideas for a little over ten years now. Sometimes I observe the spirit more than the letter of those ideas but I do this with a clear conscience in the knowledge that I'm also signposting original sources of which you can make your own sense if mine seems inadequate or unlikely.

My professional practice, and therefore the context of many of the anecdotes here, and all of the case studies, is in educational psychology. I invite you to ignore this fact and generalise everything I say to any other context you care to imagine in which it seems important to hear children's voices and understand their behaviour more clearly.

This book is *not* about therapy or counselling. I'll be inviting you to consider how PCP is highly relevant to all our lives all the time. Psychotherapy, about which Kelly wrote a great deal, is a very small part of what PCP has to offer.

This is not a 'from scratch' manual for those who find themselves working with troubled and difficult young people. I've left many gaps on the assumption that you are bringing skills and knowledge of your own.

I've tried to write in a style that is at times conversational – I hope you will find this engaging and not distracting.

If you have any prior knowledge of PCP you may be surprised to see that amongst the things I have omitted in this very short book is any mention of the repertory grid. This reflects the simple fact that the book is based on my own practice and I feel I am in good company in sharing Phillida Salmon's (1988) suspicion that the rep grid technique strays a little too far from natural conversation for comfort.

As a final thought I'd say that, unlike most other psychology, I think you are extremely unlikely to do any harm at all by knowing and using just a little PCP – quite the opposite in fact – so I invite you to read on and help fulfil my ambition to see a lot more people using a little PCP in addition to the relative few who use it a great deal. If you subsequently move from the first to the second of those groups, spread the word!

1

Introduction

What is so special about a psychologist? He experiments? Who doesn't?
He enacts his questions? Don't we all? His inquiries produce more
questions than answers: Who has ever found it to be otherwise?
(Kelly, in Maher 1969)

We are all scientists

When the psychologist George Kelly delivered the final draft of his most famous
work, *The Psychology of Personal Constructs*, to prospective publishers in the early
1950s he is said to have told friends and colleagues that he held out no hope of its
being considered fit for publication. Not only had Kelly handed over two
substantial volumes of carefully argued humanistic theory and extremely
thoroughly analysed clinical practice, but he had written at length about the
importance of listening to people's own descriptions and explanations of their
actions at a time when behaviourism was still an enormously influential paradigm
in psychology. Behaviourists then, as now, were dismissive of the suggestion that
people's thoughts and personal reflections could yield anything useful or relevant
to attempts to understand or change their behaviour. Mindful, and perhaps a
little envious, of the status and respect given to the knowledge generated by
physicists, chemists, biologists and the like, many psychologists had decided that
only observable behaviour could be deemed useful data: the kind of objective,
measurable stuff that might allow psychology to become a physics of human
beings. Thoughts, feelings and personal reflections were decidedly unwelcome
contributions to this endeavour. Against this backdrop one can appreciate the
twinkle that must surely have been in Kelly's eye when he put forward what he
liked to refer to as his 'First Principle': if you want to know what's wrong with
someone, ask him – he may tell you!

In fact, Kelly went further than asserting the importance of articulating thoughts
and feelings as part of the process of understanding behaviour. He had the
temerity to suggest, again with a degree of irreverence for his colleagues, that not

only could so-called ordinary people be trusted to describe their own lives, but that they conducted those lives in just the sort of experimental, hypothesis-testing manner that scientists had long held to be theirs alone.

The notion that each of us is to all intents and purposes a scientist, seeking to make accurate predictions about our world and then control events that take place in it, is a central idea in Kelly's work and one that this book will return to many times. 'Predict and control' might become our mantra when we assume a Kellyan perspective on human behaviour. By way of illustration, consider a common enough scenario: a young child is having a tantrum because the answer to the question 'Can I have a biscuit?' was 'No'. Personal Construct Psychology (PCP) would encourage an observer of this scene to construe the child's behaviour as much more than a simple reaction to the negative response he or she obtained. This child's behaviour is an experiment, testing the hypothesis 'If I cry then I will get a biscuit'. Perhaps this experiment produces a satisfyingly predictable result each time it is carried out: the child's harassed parent gives in and produces the required treat in order to stop the noise. When asking gets no biscuit, crying does. A dependable, 'scientific' fact has been learnt about the world! Now, one might counter this by pointing out that many young children try that ploy and get nothing at all for their pains. Well, they too have learnt something just as true about the world in which they live: crying gets you nothing (or nothing to eat at least). It follows from this just why consistency in the way adults respond to children is so important. 'Say what you mean and mean what you say' is the advice so often given to parents, teachers and others with responsibility for children's welfare and upbringing. In PCP terms it is excellent advice for it is essentially encouraging adults to make sure children get the clearest and easiest-to-interpret results from their behaviour experiments. Consider the havoc that can be wrought in a child's world by inconsistent adults. It would be analogous to the physical world conspiring to give a laboratory-based scientist a different result each time she carried out a simple measurement. Confusion and disbelief would give way to frustration and then very likely to anger. Nothing true about the world could be learnt except perhaps the need to ignore it or not to trust it. Many children and young people come to those same conclusions about the world as they see it. PCP offers a means of exploring some of the reasons why they have reached those conclusions, and a means of helping them to reach different ones.

'a unique knowledge'

More than fifty years after the publication of *The Psychology of Personal Constructs*, Kelly's ideas are arguably more popular than ever. Speculation as to why this might be could run for many more pages than this book has to spare. It certainly helps that the grip of behaviourism has been relaxed by its falling from favour as a dominant voice within the social sciences. Also, we live in an increasingly pluralist society in which the differences between us as individuals are recognised and celebrated as much as our commonalities. And perhaps most important of all is a growing awareness of the importance of empowering children by giving them a voice in discussions that would previously have only been *about* them and not in any way *with* them. This is exemplified in the United Nations Convention on the Rights of the Child, which states:

> Parties shall assure to the child who is capable of forming his or her own views the right to express those views freely in all matters affecting the child, the views of the child being given due weight in accordance with the age and maturity of the child. (UNICEF 1990, Article 12)

At a more local level the spirit of Article 12 is echoed in the following extract from the *Special Educational Needs Code of Practice*, produced by the Department for Education and Skills:

> Children and young people with special educational needs have a unique knowledge of their own needs and circumstances and their own views about what sort of help they would like … (DfES 2001)

It seems that PCP has never had more fertile ground in which to flourish. The challenge for those working and living with children and young people is to facilitate the expression of that unique knowledge and the understanding of those views. Children and young people often present us with something of a paradox: the more we appreciate their need to be heard, the harder it can be to hear them. As their situations become more complex and troubling to them, so their ability to articulate where they are and where they'd like to be may be compromised and overwhelmed. This book is aimed at anyone who'd like to hear and understand children a little better than they currently do. I think that probably means anyone who *cares* about children, which rules no one out on the basis of experience, role, qualifications or background, only on the basis of intention and aspiration. It's not a book about counselling, although it discusses techniques that might broadly be called counselling skills. Neither is it a book about therapy, although it encourages an approach to working with children that might be called therapeutic in the loosest sense of that term.

We'll proceed by first of all introducing the rich and eminently accessible theory and philosophy that underpin PCP, and then move through a series of activities that help to put the theory into practice with children and young people. It is in this last respect that I hope the book will be most useful. It has always seemed to me that this most democratic of psychologies should be able to speak and be useful to absolutely anyone with the patience to engage with it. With this in mind I've tried to take a practical, 'real world' stance on every aspect as it is discussed so that readers can make connections with their own lives and with those of children and young people that they know. In addition to the theory and practical activities, a chapter of case studies demonstrates and discusses the impact that the use of PCP has made on the lives of children and young people with whom I've worked.

I agree with Fransella and Dalton (1990): 'Understanding lies in the ability to see events through the eyes of another'. The reader who wishes to develop this ability in him- or herself will find much, I hope, of value in the chapters that follow.

2

What is Personal
Construct Psychology?

It is a psychology concerned with what we do and why we do it, rather
than one that attempts to pinpoint the events that compel others to do
what they do not choose to do. (Kelly, in Maher 1969)

Before we begin: there is an unselfconscious gender bias in Kelly's language
which is not untypical for the era in which he was writing but which nevertheless
catches the eye and ear somewhat awkwardly now. As a reader I would find
encountering [*sic*] after every example of this to be distracting, so I have not used
this device to signal my own awareness of Kelly's stylistic foibles when I cite him
directly in the text below. I hope readers will find this single acknowledgement
of the issue to be a satisfactory response.

I suppose I should preface the rest of this chapter by saying that what follows
is a personal (pun intended) interpretation of Kelly's philosophy and theory.
I'm writing about the sense I have made of Kelly's ideas in the ten years I have
been an applied psychologist, and the use I have been able to make of them, in
the hope that this will inspire and energise others to begin a relationship with
this most illuminating of psychologies. At times I will skip very lightly over
sections of Kelly's theoretical arguments and I will do so without apology
because I firmly believe that even an edited and reduced Kelly can be mined for
greater riches than the complete works of many other psychologists. There's
no question that, for the fullest and most detailed picture, anyone with any
interest in PCP should read Kelly's arguments in the original texts and then
follow the development of those ideas through the books and papers about
PCP published by others. The references at the back of this book give some
useful starting points. But much of that detail can be acquired *after* the 'big
picture' has been assimilated, and it's that 'big picture' that I want to deal with
now. But first some reflection time.

Some personal reflection

Before we go any further, let's try an exercise that I often ask participants in PCP training sessions to take part in because it sets the scene very neatly for discussion of one of Kelly's most important ideas.

The exercise is simply this: picture yourself in your best-case and worst-case scenarios. When and where do you feel at your absolute best, at your most comfortable? What are you doing? What's happening around you? Who is there with you? Conversely, ask yourself these same questions about what would be a 'nightmare' scenario for you. In both cases let me emphasise that I'm not asking you to fantasise or conjure up a surreal nightmare scene for yourself – rather, these should be plausible things that either have happened or could happen to you. I'd encourage you to make a note of what you've imagined because we will come back to it after we've taken a first look at some Personal Construct theory.

George Kelly's three 'big ideas'

I'm going to argue that there are really three 'big ideas' in PCP as originally described by George Kelly. The first (in no particular order) is the existence in our heads, in our thinking, of things called constructs. Closely related to this is

the philosophical standpoint that Kelly called 'constructive alternativism' – an optimistic view of life in which the possibilities for change are limited only by the possibility of imagining change. The third idea is the centrality in human lives of the need for prediction and control of events around us.

Let's start with a close look at constructs: the role they play in everyday thought and the extent to which they enable us to appreciate the many possible ways of perceiving the world around us.

What is a construct?

At the simplest level we might call a construct an either/or verbal tool that helps us to make sense of the world. Kelly argued very clearly that much of our perception of objects and experiences falls into relatively simple dichotomies: good/bad, right/wrong, light/dark, happy/unhappy and so on. For example, before you bought this book you may have wondered whether it was going to be useful or a waste of money; you might now be finding its contents illuminating or possibly mundane; you might feel it is well-written or perhaps heavy-going. In PCP terms we would say that those three contrasting judgements are all constructs that could conceivably be in the head of anyone choosing to describe a piece of non-fiction writing:

Useful .... Waste of money

Illuminating .... Mundane

Well-written .... Heavy-going

Of course, you'd be unlikely to say both ends (or 'poles') of each construct out loud when giving your opinion about the book. In conversation you'd be more likely to say, perhaps:

Well, it was heavy-going at times but once I got into it I found it very illuminating. Overall, definitely a useful book from my point of view.

Those descriptive terms aren't constructs but they are the beginnings of constructs. I'd have to ask you some more questions to reveal the rest of the construct – the term at the other end, or *contrast pole* as it is properly known. We'll come back to the topic of eliciting constructs later. For now I just want you to feel that you have a grasp of what a construct looks like when we reveal it and how it relates to the everyday business of making sense of the world.

Let's look at how constructs function in an area much closer to many children's experiences – persistent literacy difficulties.

Where do *you* stand in the 'great dyslexia debate'? Does it even exist? If so, what causes it and what should be done to support children who have dyslexia? Some people think that dyslexia is a symptom of underlying neurological deficits in the brains of certain children. Underpinning this view is (amongst other things) a construct that must look something like this:

Children with dyslexia .... Children with normal brains

Others feel that the evidence suggests a skill deficit rather than a neurological one. Their construct about dyslexia looks more like this:

Children with dyslexia .... Children with good phonological skills

It often seems to me that constructs are rather like icebergs. One pole bobs above the waterline giving very little clue as to what lies below. In both constructs above we find the word 'dyslexia' being used but this is merely the tip of the iceberg – we don't know what the fuller implications of that term are for the person using it until we know what they contrast dyslexia with; we need to know what they would call children who don't have dyslexia. This is much more than playing with words. The implications of each construct for the children and young people it applies to are very different indeed. Phonological skills can be taught by teachers and parents but what will we do about children whose brains are unlike those of their typically developing peers? Solutions to their difficulties may lie in the hands of professionals with skills that might seem increasingly remote from those who live and work with these children on a daily basis. And how might children's motivation to learn to read be affected by the sense *they* make of these different explanations of their literacy difficulties? Working to overcome neurological problems must feel very different to trying to play catch-up with skills of phonology.

On the other hand, there are those who feel that dyslexia doesn't exist as a discrete condition at all and that there are merely

Children who can't read well .... Children who can read well

When they try to debate the issue with those whose professional practice is built around the following construct (amongst others):

Children with dyslexia .... Children who don't have dyslexia

the debate can become fraught because the two constructs are mutually exclusive. And for maximum controversy we might note that there is also a view of children's literacy difficulties that would see most of the above labelled as misguided and inappropriate. This view is underpinned by the construct that there are

Children who have been taught well .... Children who have been taught badly

In other words, we should stop 'blaming' children and construing their inability to read as indicative of any kind of deficit in them and instead we should construe their 'failure' to acquire literacy skills as evidence of our failure to teach them sufficiently well. Clearly the finite resources available for the education of our children would be deployed very differently by someone for whom that construct seemed valid and useful as opposed to the one above it.

I've scratched the surface of some of the debates about dyslexia only as a means of revealing some of the constructs underpinning them and in order to show those constructs at work – influencing perception, thought and behaviour. To keep us grounded I'm going to give the last word to a young man I met who was struggling very hard to learn to read and was acutely aware of his difficulties. One of his constructs about himself will remind us, if any reminder is needed, of the reason why it still matters that we engage with the debates about literacy, despite the complexities and contradictions that they throw up:

Thick* .... Good at reading+

* where I am now
+ where I'd like to be

Constructive alternativism:
what does it mean to 'reconstrue' something?

Kelly's philosophical position of constructive alternativism invites us to believe that one can change one's world in a significant way by changing how one construes any part of it.

> ... *all of our present interpretations of the universe are subject to revision or replacement* ... there are always some alternative constructions available to choose among in dealing with the world. No one needs to paint himself into a corner; ... no one needs to be the victim of his biography.
> (Kelly 1955; emphasis in original)

It's an attractive philosophy but how is it possible to do this? Nearly all of the literature about PCP deals with this issue at some length because it is such an important part of Kelly's theory. Burr and Butt (1992) devote four chapters of their book to a very accessible discussion of the issue, seeking to ground it in everyday questions and dilemmas. I'm going to concentrate here on two different ways of articulating constructive alternativism that I think are relevant to working with children and to all our lives on a daily basis; two ways, that is, of reconstruing people, events, experiences, ideas and emotions within the language of PCP.

(1) Challenging and changing constructs

Fransella and Dalton (1990) have a nice example of the way in which a change to one pole of a construct can have profound consequences for the individual who uses it. Think how differently the world would be perceived by two people who both enjoy the company of friends but whose constructs about friendship differ as follows:

Person A: Friend .... Enemy

Person B: Friend .... Acquaintance

If you don't become a friend of Person A then he considers you to be his enemy. If you don't become a friend of Person B she'll consider you merely an acquaintance. Imagine their different reactions to meeting new people for the first time.

I was once asked to do some coaching work with a newly qualified teacher in a secondary school who had requested support to develop her practice around classroom management and control. Charlotte was struggling to stay sufficiently 'in charge' of the classes she taught to ensure that she could teach and her pupils could learn.

In our first meeting I asked Charlotte to describe herself – what kind of teacher was she exactly? She said she felt that, amongst other things, she was a 'cheerful' teacher and contrasted this with 'boring' – a word that applied, in her opinion, to some of her colleagues in school.

Cheerful .... Boring

What appears on the face of it to be a fairly harmless construct turned out to lie at the heart of the difficulties that Charlotte was having. Charlotte's need to project a cheerful persona in the classroom was a core value for her as a teacher and she associated 'strict' classroom control only with boring teachers. Charlotte strongly wanted her pupils to like her and to enjoy her company. Unfortunately, because she had developed a view that cheerful teachers didn't remonstrate with pupils for fear of damaging relationships with them, the young people she was teaching were able to take advantage of Charlotte's good-natured approach and get away with doing very little work.

What seemed to be holding back the development of Charlotte's practice was a disproportionate investment on her part in the importance of being cheerful, driven by a desperate need to avoid being boring. Unfortunately, this was at the expense of classroom management skills that were inextricably linked with the 'boring' approach she so wanted to avoid. Charlotte's cheerful/boring construct was actually this one in disguise:

Cheerful teachers .... Teachers with good classroom control

For a while Charlotte was resistant to the notion that any systematic classroom management strategies, any attempt on her part to 'impose' her authority on the class, could help children to learn any more effectively than a 'cheerful' approach to building relationships with them. Charlotte seemed to have developed this view during her teacher training and it appeared to have served her well then, but was not doing so now. What was needed was to untangle 'boring' from 'good classroom control'. To do this we needed to focus our discussion of teaching away from constructs about specific personality attributes and instead find a construct that would allow us to discuss the 'point' of being a teacher in the first place – why would anyone do it? Charlotte was very clear that teaching was about making a difference to pupils' lives, to help them learn and grow. We were now discussing

Teachers who make a difference .... Teachers who don't make a difference

What do 'teachers who make a difference' do to ensure the best outcomes for their pupils? Could Charlotte remember teachers who made a difference to her – what did they do, how did they behave? Charlotte conceded that her memories of 'teachers who make a difference' included people who had been 'strict' in terms of classroom control but had also been the kind of 'cheerful' teacher that she wanted to be. In being able to reconstrue cheerfulness as not incompatible with classroom control Charlotte had taken a small but significant step. That's not to say that changing her practice was then easy, but she became someone who could at least begin to reconstruct her model of good teaching in a way that allowed her to be the kind of teacher she wanted to be and helped her to be the kind of teacher her pupils needed.

(2) Changing places: moving constructs around

Here's one of the many different constructs I use for making sense of people:

Good listener .... Ignorant

If I ever meet you, and we talk at some length, one of the many decisions that I might make about you is whether you seem to me to be a good listener or whether you're not a good listener and are therefore in my opinion an ignorant person. Notice that constructs are rarely about dictionary-definition opposites. My construct *isn't* 'Good listener … Bad listener'. It's a good deal subtler and more revealing of my thinking than that, as are most constructs. Hear me describe someone as a good listener and you'll get a modest insight into my thinking. Clearly I value good listening, but then again who doesn't? But when you discover that I contrast good listening with ignorance – when you uncover one of my personal constructs in other words – you have a much more powerful and revealing glimpse of one of the tools that I use to make sense of the world. After all, it is a very personal and idiosyncratic decision of mine to construe people who aren't good listeners as ignorant. Any number of other descriptions might apply to such people – what do *you* call people who aren't good listeners?

Kelly reminds us that at any one time, in any one moment of perception and anticipation, only a few of our constructs are needed. Each construct is in fact only fit for certain purposes. Constructs that might help me to recognise a lifelong partner will be different to those I might use to choose a window-cleaner. And none of those constructs would be much help to me if I were trying to understand the behaviour of atoms and molecules. At the same time, constructs about partners and window-cleaners clearly all belong to a group that I find useful for understanding people. Kelly suggested that our constructs are shuffled into some sort of order within a hierarchical system. Because construing is a dynamic and fluid process then no fixed map of my or your construct system could ever be possible, but if I reflect a little more on my Good listener/Ignorant construct I can pin it down to a rough position in the

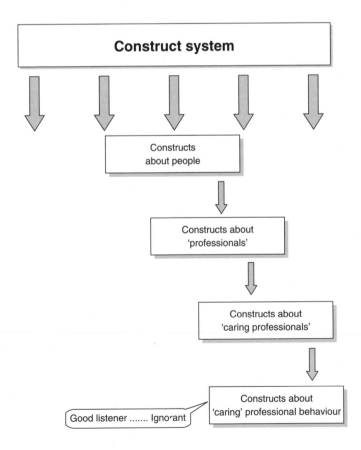

hierarchy that shows, amongst other things, when I would and wouldn't find it a helpful construct to use.

It turns out that my Good listener/Ignorant construct is *not* a tool for making judgements about people in general. If you and I meet socially I may never think those thoughts about you. It's not even a construct that I find useful when thinking about professional people. But if I meet you in a professional capacity and you are a member of what I perceive to be a 'caring', person-orientated profession then I will at some point begin to rattle you down one or other end of the Good listener/Ignorant dichotomy.

It doesn't matter that it's a hopelessly complex task even to try to accurately map your own or anyone else's construct system in the way I've very tentatively started above. What's important, and particularly so when we're attempting to reconstrue, is to try to get a rough sense of a particular construct's position within someone's thinking. It can be a source of much confusion, misunderstanding and even unhappiness to try to press a construct into service in a place where it's just not fit for purpose. Let's think about the likely outcomes if my Good listener/ Ignorant construct were located in a more superordinate position within the hierarchy in, say, 'Constructs about people'.

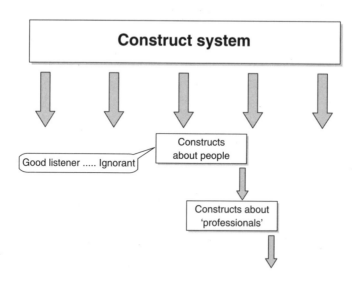

What's happened here is that rather than judging only caring professionals by the Good listener/Ignorant criterion, I'm now judging absolutely everyone I meet in that way. Under these circumstances I could very quickly become impatient and angry with my next-door neighbour, the bus driver, my children and a host of other people who would be at the very least bemused to detect themselves being judged by a criterion not appropriate to their relationship with me. What I hope this illustrates is that sometimes there may be no need at all to challenge or change a construct in order to reconstrue the world, merely a need to wonder if it would function better in a different place. For me, Good listener/Ignorant works best when it's tucked away for a specific purpose, not pressed into service on a daily basis.

Although we're quite immersed in the theory of PCP at the moment, I think we know the above to be true intuitively. Two further examples: after the best part of a century of debate and controversy about the value of IQ measurement, the Intelligent/Unintelligent construct is gradually being relocated for most us (that is to say, those of us who were ever interested in such things in the first place) from our 'Constructs about people' to our 'Constructs about behaviour', where it can cause far less mischief. Similarly, when I say I construe you as a friend, part of what that means is that my thoughts and judgements about you are guided by constructs that cluster in that part of my system which deals with friends and friendship, not business transaction, line management, or family obligation. If our friendship is mutual and equally rewarding for both of us then the chances are that your constructs about friends and friendship are similar to mine and are in a similar position in your overall system.

Behaviour as hypothesis-testing: the need for prediction and control

> … every man is, in his own particular way, a scientist.

> Now what would happen if we were to reopen the question of human motivation and use our long-range view of man to infer just what it is that sets the course of his endeavour?... Might not the individual man, each in his own personal way, assume more of the stature of a scientist, ever seeking to predict and control the course of events with which he is involved? (Kelly 1955)

Why does Kelly think it is fruitful to see human motivation and behaviour in this way? He was very alert to what he saw as the paradox of only so-called 'scientists' being construed (and construing themselves) as purposeful, rational, experimental and meaning-seeking, whilst the rest of us (non-scientists) apparently behave as we do because of a cocktail of irresistible forces such as our upbringing, our relationship with our mothers or fathers, our experiences of reward and punishment, our genetic inheritance and so on. Kelly argues that ordinary human behaviour is every bit as rational as a scientific experiment *when understood on its own terms*. In PCP, behaviour is seen as experimental and hypothesis-testing; it 'makes sense' in a way that is perfectly logical to the person doing the behaving even if it makes no sense at all to anyone else. This is a very important point and we need to unpack it in some more detail.

I don't want us to get hung up now on detailed debate about the nature of scientific enquiry. Kelly is *not* suggesting that you and I live our lives enacting the kind of double-blind controlled procedures that are the gold standard of the experimental method in the scientific community. He just wanted to construct an argument for viewing men and women as active meaning-makers with a hypothesis-testing stance to the world around them. We'll turn later to look at how those hypotheses are formed in the first place. For now I'll try to present the argument that Kelly makes for viewing behaviour as the everyday equivalent of a scientific experiment – the means by which theories and hypotheses are *tested*. Let me also say before we go any further that I don't see this as a question of trying to convince you that Kelly's ideas are 'true' and that this is how people 'really' think. I don't believe any theory of human psychology can sensibly lay claim to an exclusive, objective truth about people. Rather, it's more about whether our understanding of human behaviour is helpfully illuminated by construing it in the way Kelly suggests. The question is simply this: does the notion of 'man as scientist' trying to predict and control events around him help us to make sense of people's behaviour? If we feel it does then arguments about its 'truth' are irrelevant.

Scientists rarely, if ever, launch themselves and their work into the complete unknown. Rather, they proceed much more cautiously, devising experiments derived from theories that encapsulate their best understandings of past events observed. I'm simplifying somewhat here, but we might see the scientific method as a sequence like this:

> Observation – theory – hypothesis – experiment –
> observation – theory (adjusted) – hypothesis –
> experiment – observation – etc.

The goal of this sequence is simply to find out something 'true' about the world. I'm sure it's uncontroversial to point out that the whole sequence is driven by questions: Why? What? How? and so on. I think the most common question motivating scientific experiments is this one:

I should make it clear that by 'experiment' I mean an *activity* designed to find something out, as opposed to, say, an observation or some speculation, both of which are passive pursuits that don't require interaction with the world. Any good theory allows and encourages predictions to be made in answer to the above question. Indeed, all theories have predictions contained within them – if they didn't they'd just be descriptions and not theories at all. Experiments are used to test predictions, usually formulated as hypotheses, and in so doing to test also the robustness of the theory those predictions are derived from. Depending on the results observed, the theory may need tweaking or adjustment. With luck (or more likely good judgement!) the theory becomes better and better at answering the question 'What will happen if …?' and in this way theories also accrue practical applications – we know what will happen in the world around us if we do certain things in a certain way. A very important corollary of 'knowing what will happen next' is a sense of being in control. If, like the successful scientist, you can make sound predictions, if you are confident what the consequences of your actions will be, if you have certain knowledge of what the immediate future holds, then you will feel you have some control over the events occurring around you.

… there are various ways in which the world is construed. Some of them are undoubtedly better than others. They are better from our human point of view because they support more precise and more accurate predictions about more events. (Kelly 1955)

So, the scientific experiment is a purposeful, logical activity designed to find out something about the world in which the experiment occurs so that ultimately the scientist can feel ever more confident in his or her ability to predict and control what goes on around them. How does any of the above apply to children and young people, and to you and me in our everyday lives? Let me give you some examples from my own experience and then we'll look at some from yours.

As I wrote some of the above paragraphs this morning my 11-month-old son, Joe, made a bid for some of my breakfast. He'd already had his and was finishing up by chewing on a rice cake. I had some toast, which he likes very much, and he wanted some of mine. The question for him was clearly: how to get some toast instead of rice cake? Below is how he went about it and I am indeed suggesting that this was purposeful, hypothesis-testing, 'experimental' behaviour on his part, with a view to finding out something 'true' and important about the world.

The answer to the second question is: nothing much. So the question becomes:

The answer this time is: some noises and lots of attention from me, including return of the rice cake, but still no toast. So the next question is:

The answer to that question is, sadly for him: more noises and attention from me but still no toast. Instead I wave the rice cake around in front of him. Fortunately his next thought seems to be:

Might as well eat this rice cake then.

Which is good news from my point of view because I've got a pretty good idea by now that it's my toast he's after and I know for a fact that I don't want him to think he can get some by throwing his food around and kicking up a fuss. When his rice cake is finished I offer him some toast. He accepts of course!

What have his behaviour experiments taught him? For a start, no amount of throwing or shouting gets you what you want but, as far as food is concerned, if you finish what you've got you might get a little bit of something else you want. In the place where he lives that's a scientific fact!

Of course Joe's too young to tell us what he's thinking. But that doesn't matter because, as I said above, it's not a question of what he's 'really' thinking but rather of whether it's *illuminating* in any way to see him as experimenting with different ways to get toast instead of rice cake. And if it is, how is it helpful to him and to those who care for him to see his behaviour in this way?

My feeling is that it *is* particularly illuminating to see children's behaviour in this way because it suggests to us that the behaviours that sometimes annoy, puzzle or stress us are almost always trying to solve a problem, not create one. Much other psychology has left us too often viewing children as reacting to events rather than, as Kelly urges, anticipating them. Parents and carers have a unique opportunity to help shape very young children's lives. So much of children's relationship with the world around them is bound up with their relationship with their primary carers. Let's push the 'experimental' analogy one step further: for my 11-month-old son a big part of the 'data' that his behaviour experiments produce depends on the responses from me and his mum. We can help shape what he learns in many situations by making sure his experiments get results that we're comfortable with and that are in his best interests. Now, just as a scientist can only feel confident that they have learnt something true and dependable about the world if they always get the same result from the same experiment, so it is for children; those whose confidence grows the most are those who get reassuringly predictable results from their behaviour experiments. Adults have to be consistent and predictable. Say what you mean and mean what you say.

> ### Consistent = predictable = reassuring
> This kind of reassurance allows children to test out their ideas and learn 'true' things about the world

Meet Hannah. She's 10 years old and attends a primary school just down the road from where she lives with her mum and two sisters.

If you ask her, and she trusts you, Hannah will tell you that she doesn't have any friends. If you were to observe Hannah at school you'd very likely come to the conclusion that she's a bit of a loner. Most children and adults seem to take no notice of her. Hannah hasn't previously been in much trouble at school but this year she is getting into trouble on an almost daily basis for 'silly' behaviour. This can include pinching and thumping children who are sitting nearby, calling out while the teacher is talking, throwing things like pencils and pens across the room and leaving her seat for no good reason when she's supposed to be getting on with her work.

In Hannah's school children are grouped by ability for some lessons. As is the way in primary schools, children stay with their main class-teacher for most of each day but move into a different class for an hour or so each day for a particular lesson with the rest of their ability group. The odd thing about Hannah's behaviour is that when she goes to a different class to do her numeracy work, with a different teacher, she never misbehaves. All of Hannah's 'silly' behaviour occurs back in class with her usual teacher.

There are lots of possible explanations for this. Does she like maths? Not particularly. Is she good at maths, even if she doesn't like it? No; Hannah actually struggles with maths work and her group is the lowest ability one. Does she like the other children in her maths group better than the children in her class? Not really; her maths group seems to be as indifferent to Hannah as the other children are. Is the maths group smaller than the normal class size she's used to? No, the ability groups have been worked out to be about the same size as the classes.

If you ask Hannah why she gets into trouble in her class but not in her maths group she will say 'Don't know'. It is a tough question to answer after all (but certainly worth asking, as Kelly himself would have pointed out). However, observe Hannah in her class and then also in her maths group and you might develop a theory about why her behaviour changes. Hannah's class-teacher, Mrs P, is a kind person who quite clearly goes out of her way to try to make every day and every lesson interesting for the children. Mrs P's enthusiasm often outstrips her organization skills, however, with the consequence that her lessons can be a little chaotic. Sometimes she appears to find the chaos energizing; at other times Mrs P seems to be exasperated by it. Children are not always clear about what they have to do, and they are certainly not always clear about what they have to do to be successful in response to the work challenges that Mrs P sets.

By contrast, Mrs B, who teaches Hannah's maths ability group, runs that lesson with something akin to military precision. Children are acknowledged and greeted individually as they enter the room. They sit according to a seating plan and can start work immediately because Mrs B ensures that a task that the children can access independently is always ready and waiting for them on each table. There are written rules and positive expectations posted up in her room and she often refers to them as she teaches and talks to the children. Mrs B seems to have eyes in the back of her head and if you step over the line of what's acceptable to her you soon know it, but to be fair she is as quick to spot good behaviour as she is to deal with transgressions.

If you ask her, Hannah will call Mrs B 'strict' and Mrs P 'nice'. Talk to her in more detail about those terms and she will say that a 'strict' teacher is one who doesn't let you get away with anything. A 'nice' teacher is someone who never shouts at you. Although she's not as 'nice' as Mrs P, Hannah would like to be in Mrs B's class all the time. Hannah finds it hard to say why, particularly given that she feels Mrs P is 'nice'.

Hannah leaves us to speculate on why she might prefer to be in a different teacher's class, and why her behaviour is so different in the two different classes. What is the essential difference between Mrs P and Mrs B? In Personal Construct terms we would note that Mrs B is a far more predictable person than Mrs P and that from Hannah's perspective this predictability must be a good thing. To use two familiar phrases, Mrs P continually 'moves the goalposts', but 'you know where you stand' with Mrs B. We mustn't oversimplify Hannah's needs in the interests of neatness of discussion but she seems to be particularly sensitive to the lack of certainty around how to behave and succeed in her own class. Mrs P's inconsistent responses to the children she works with seem to put Hannah in constant 'experimental' or 'hypothesis-testing' mode: What happens if I say this? What happens if I throw that? How do I get this to happen? How do I avoid this happening? etc. Because Mrs P seems barely ever to do the same thing the same way twice it's virtually impossible to learn anything 'true' about how to be a good, or bad, pupil in her class. It's not clear how to impress Mrs P; it's not clear how to please her. It's not even clear how to annoy her! So despite her basic friendliness and good intentions it's actually rather unsettling to be left in Mrs P's care, and for a child not very confident about the rights and wrongs of the world (we might assume that includes Hannah), Mrs P's very mixed messages are not useful ways of learning more about it. Crucially, because Hannah can never be quite sure what response she'll get from Mrs P, time spent in her company is time when Hannah's mental and physical wellbeing must feel as if they are entirely in her teacher's hands and beyond her own control; a very uncomfortable feeling indeed. In Mrs B's class children know what to do to get a certain sort of response (good or bad) from her. This effectively helps those children to feel they have some control over their immediate environment and over the things that will happen to them. Like scientists, they can reflect on the reassuringly predictable results of their (behaviour) experiments and feel that they are learning 'true' things about their world. In PCP terms we would see Hannah's 'silly' behaviour as an attempt to both understand her world and to bring it under her control.

Kelly suggested that each individual construct in a person's system plays a small part in helping that person to be an accurate predictor of events around them. He used the term 'predictive efficiency' to label the extent to which any construct offered a chance to see the world clearly and accurately. Constructs with good predictive efficiency allow the construer to make sound predictions about what is likely to happen next in their world. Those with poor predictive efficiency will often mislead and cause people, actions and situations to be misconstrued. We'll finish this overview of the theory behind PCP by looking at an example of the effects of differing levels of predictive efficiency before returning finally to your own personal reflections from the beginning of this chapter.

I had a female friend once who declared, after a number of unhappy relationships, 'All men are inherently ridiculous.' I hope you'll agree with me that that's not a very accurate statement. The construct it reveals would probably look something like this:

Men .... Sensible people

In other words, you can be a man or you can be sensible but you can't be both. Pretty harsh in its blanket dismissal of half the world's population! In PCP terms we would say that this construct has poor predictive efficiency because, frankly, the construer will often be wrong in the judgments she makes about men. She will have to ignore or fail to perceive a great deal of positive behaviour on their part in order to maintain this construct in her thinking. I like to use a visual analogy and think of this as like looking at a blurred picture. My friend was looking at the same 'picture' as everyone else (i.e. men and their behaviour) but her picture was so distorted that her ideas about what it contained became very unreliable.

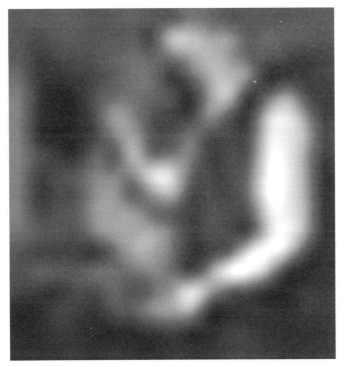

Poor predictive efficiency – 'All men are ridiculous.'

A slightly more moderate view, although still rather sweeping and dismissive, would be 'Some people are ridiculous.' The construct implied by this view would look like this:

Ridiculous people .... Sensible people

We might suggest that this construct has a fair degree of predictive efficiency. It's slightly more realistic than judging others purely on the basis of gender but it's still a rather blunt instrument and will encourage a pigeon-holing approach to the perception of others – you're either always ridiculous or always sensible, full stop! In our visual analogy the detail nevertheless becomes a little clearer.

Fair predictive efficiency – 'Some people are ridiculous.'

A more finely graded way of looking at the world would be the view that everyone is capable of acting in a ridiculous manner sometimes. It's not a case of all men being ridiculous, nor is it fair to say that some people are ridiculous all the time; it's simply the case that anyone you care to mention will probably do something ridiculous at least once in their life. The construct underpinning this world-view would be:

Ridiculous behaviour .... Sensible behaviour

Arguably this is a construct that will offer a far better chance of seeing the world clearly, or the least chance of distorting one's perception of the world such that only a partial picture can be seen. The construer will not rush into blanket condemnations of people on first sight, nor will they inflexibly insist that any one person will be likely to behave in the same way all the time. This construct will support a wide variety of predictions – it opens up many possibilities in perceiving the world and it closes down very few. In our visual analogy the details are now revealed fully.

Good predictive efficiency – 'Bob sometimes behaves ridiculously.'

Reflecting on your reflections

Think back to your responses to the personal reflection exercise I asked you to try at the start of this chapter. What are your 'best-case' and 'worst-case' scenarios?

If Kelly is right to suggest that it is a fundamental human need to be in constant pursuit of predictability and control then your personal reflections in response to the questions I asked should show some clear evidence of this. It should be the case that at the heart of your best- and worst-case scenarios are issues of prediction and control. Is that the case? I have certainly found it to be so on the many occasions when I've been able to get immediate feedback from people who have engaged with this activity. People's best scenarios usually revolve around familiar places and familiar routines or activities. These are times and circumstances when things follow a reassuringly predictable pattern. People often visualise themselves amongst close family and/or friends. Interestingly, it's also not uncommon for people to be alone in a particular environment. By contrast, the worst scenarios see people in circumstances they cannot control and amongst others whose actions are hard or impossible to predict. Examples I have been given in the past have included dealing with a loved one's illness, public speaking, mountaineering and childbirth! On the face of it they could hardly have less in common as a set of experiences but a PCP perspective allows them all to be seen as united by the common thread of loss of control. I think it only adds to the value of Kelly's insight that one person's nightmare scenario can indeed be another's optimum one. Public speaking is a good example – it is not an activity in which loss of control by the speaker is inevitable; many speakers are very confident that they can 'take an audience with them'. Their confidence that this will be the case will no doubt correlate very strongly with their sense of control over the outcomes of the activity. Mountaineering would be another case in point: I would not be surprised to hear an experienced and confident mountaineer say that being in a situation that to others would seem perilous would be to them absolute bliss. Perceptions of one's own ability to impact on a situation and take a reasonable amount of control of what happens in that situation are key – for this reason some folk would certainly rather climb a mountain than try to make small talk with strangers at a party.

3

How do you 'do' Personal Construct Psychology?

Personal construct psychology lays stress on the ability to try things out, to think in hypothetical and provisional ways. We learn, not by seeking to find some absolute truth, but by exploring where ideas lead ... (Salmon 1995)

We have discussed constructs at some length but this has remained at a largely theoretical level. We now need to deal very practically with them. In this chapter we'll look at ways of talking to and working with children and young people that encourage them to offer the small glimpses into their world-view that we, with their help, can identify as constructs. We can then explore those constructs in some detail – their implications and influence on behaviour – and show how a better understanding of someone's construing of the world can help others to support them if support is needed.

There are many ways in which one can explore children's construing and I don't pretend for a minute to say that what follows represents a comprehensive overview. If we say that our starting point is simply the desire to find out more about how children see themselves and the world around them, then it's obvious that there are innumerable ways of approaching that goal. We'll take as our focus here methods that in my own practice I have found to be very accessible and fruitful: three activities designed to elicit personal constructs and three activities for exploring them in detail. As well as Kelly (1955) I've found Bannister and Fransella (1986) and Fransella and Dalton (1990) very useful on issues of both construct elicitation and exploration, including Laddering and Pyramiding. Phillida Salmon (1988) of course takes the credit for Salmon Lines.

Just as I am making no claims here of exhaustive analysis of PCP practice, neither am I suggesting that the activities that follow should be construed *on their own* as sufficient attempts to engage with children's wider experiences. Chapter 7 and the CD Rom accompanying this book hopefully make that clear by embedding work specifically focused on constructs within the broader conversational framework of the Let's Talk programme.

Eliciting constructs

The process of revealing some of your constructs can be a very simple one – I just need to hear you describe something. To illustrate this, let's return briefly to the example I gave in Chapter 2 of someone 'reviewing' this book. Imagine that I had given you an early draft to read. A week later I asked how you found the book and you told me that the book was 'exciting'. Now at the moment this is not a construct – it's just an adjective, albeit one that is already giving us some insight into your thinking (the fact that you are someone who can be excited by non-fiction books is certainly interesting). With one quite innocuous additional question I can transform this descriptive term into a construct and reveal something with much richer implications for your thinking and behaviour. The question is simply this: 'What would you call a book that *isn't* exciting?' Let's imagine that after a little thought you reply 'Ordinary'. We have our first complete construct from you:

Exciting .... Ordinary

That is to say that we now know you're someone for whom books are (amongst other things) either exciting or ordinary. In the terminology of PCP we would call 'exciting' the **emergent pole** of the construct – the part that is first revealed to us. In this case the emergent pole was revealed in response to a direct question that we put to you but it could as easily have been in something you wrote (a published book review, an email, a letter) or it could have cropped up in a conversation that we merely overheard. By asking you to tell us what you call books that *aren't* exciting we obtain from you the **contrast pole** of the construct, in this case 'ordinary'. With the emergent pole and the contrast pole side by side we have revealed one of your personal constructs.

So far, so good, but I don't often want to know how people feel about non-fiction books. I'm much more interested in exploring how people think about and make sense of people. Specifically, I like to know what sense they make of themselves and their own situations. To begin this process I need someone to describe him- or herself. Kelly discusses a method of eliciting this which he calls self-characterization. This involves asking someone to write about him- or herself in the third person. In my work with children and young people I have invariably found that this task, as originally formulated, asks a little too much of them, principally, I think, because it can feel more like a chore than a voyage of self-discovery. Literacy difficulties, when present, clearly also compound the issue. This is not a problem, however, as I have found that the following much-reduced version of Kelly's task can still be very fruitful.

How would you describe yourself?

My experience suggests that from the age of about seven years children are increasingly confident about responding to this challenge but some elaboration or mediation of the basic question is required, particularly for younger children. I am aware that over the course of many conversations I have developed something of a loose script in my head to help children to respond successfully to this question. The following is offered as an example of the way in which I word and re-word this question to make it accessible to children. Terms such as 'personality', 'character' and even 'phrases' may not always be completely understood by some children but by re-wording the question in a number of ways I find that I can convey the sense of what I'm asking clearly enough. It's not my intention to be prescriptive here though; clearly some judgement and differentiation of language is needed according to the age and maturity of the child one is talking to.

> Imagine someone wanted to get to know you really well but they'd never met you before. This person says 'What's [child's name] like? What kind of personality has s/he got, what kind of character is s/he?' Now, *you* get to answer those questions, you're the one who decides what this person finds out about you. But the challenge for you is this: you can only pick 5 or 6 words to describe yourself – 5 or 6 different describing words or short phrases to say what you're really like. Try to give them a true picture of the kind of person you are. If you were trying to be really honest about yourself what words would you pick?

The following is a selection of things children and young people have said to me when I have asked them to describe themselves. Any suspicion that they will always want to paint themselves in as favourable a light as possible, or that they will offer bland responses with no emotional commitment, is very rarely justified in my experience.

- naughty
- need help with behaviour
- angry
- strange
- disabled
- intimidating
- funny
- loud

- like mucking about
- chubby build
- friendly
- active
- not normal
- geek
- friendless

Each response is an emergent pole of a construct, of course. As described in the example about non-fiction books above, the most straightforward way of obtaining the contrast pole is to ask 'What would you call someone who isn't …?'. When I asked Euan what he would call someone who isn't 'naughty' he said 'good'. When I asked Tim what he would call people who aren't 'intimidating' he said they would 'keep themselves to themselves'. Annie told me that she would be 'popular' if she wasn't a 'geek'.

I have found that one also needs to be prepared to present this second question in a number of different ways in order to ensure that children understand what's being asked of them. My script for this includes any combination of the following that is required until a confident response is forthcoming:

> What would you call someone who isn't naughty? … So, there are naughty people and there are people who are …? … You've said that you're naughty; what word would you use for people who really aren't like you? … You've been very honest and said you're naughty; can you think of someone who isn't naughty? What word would you use to describe him/her?

Although it's tempting, avoid at all costs asking 'What's the *opposite of* naughty?' That effectively just reduces the question to a kind of verbal reasoning test and there's no saying that the answer you will get is the contrast pole. For example, if you ask me what the opposite of naughty is I might say 'good', but if you ask me what I call someone who isn't naughty I'll say 'boring'. A much more interesting and personal response. If you want to elicit *constructs* don't ask for opposites!

Triadic elicitation

Another means of revealing constructs is triadic elicitation. A method for this that I often use is as follows: a carefully folded and cut or torn piece of A4 paper will give eight very serviceable rectangular 'cards' on each of which the child is asked to write the name of a friend, family member or very familiar person. It's not essential but I often ask children to put themselves on one of the cards so that they are one of the eight. When the cards are complete a random selection of three of them is placed in front of the child who is then asked 'Is there anything that two of these people have got in common that isn't true about the other person?' Other possibilities for framing this question are as follows:

> In what way are two of these people alike but the other one different? … Is there a way in which two of these people are the same and the other person is not like that at all? … Is there something that is true about two of these people that is not true about the third one?

Below is an example of what that might look like in practice, and a flavour of the dialogue that might accompany it. Repeat this same procedure as many times as is necessary in order to elicit constructs that you feel will reward further exploration. Any combination of three names can be used; as well as random selections you should offer the child or young person a chance to pick three and you might pick three. You may have a good reason for wanting to ensure that a particular combination of names comes up.

Mum   John   Sanjeev

> Is there some way in which two of these people are alike which means they're different to the other one? Is there something that two of them have got in common and the other one hasn't?

> *Well, John and Sanjeev like to have a laugh but Mum's usually pretty serious.*

> Okay, let's try another three names.

Charlie   Dad   Baby Henry

> What about these three? What have two of them got in common that isn't true for the third one?

> *Charlie and Baby Henry are both noisy! Dad just leaves me alone and lets me have some peace and quiet.*

And what about these ones? How are two of them alike?

Mum and Alfie both get cross and shout sometimes.

And if you're not like that, what do you do?

I stay quiet.

As should be clear from this, provided the child you're working with feels able to answer the basic question about similarity and difference, one rather neat consequence of triadic elicitation is the revealing of both poles of a construct at the same time. The relatively brief dialogue above has already elicited three different constructs that tell us, even without further exploration, some interesting things about how the construer looks at the different people around them:

Like to have a laugh .... Pretty serious

Noisy people .... People who leave me alone

Get cross .... Stay quiet

It's worth giving some thought to variations on the basic task of selecting the names that go on the cards. If you particularly want to investigate issues about friendship and peer interactions then it might be beneficial to insist that only the names of children or young people known to the child you're working with go on the cards. You might want to ensure that only close family members' names are used if constructs about family relationships are wanted. Another variation would be asking the child to choose and include people very remote from them – film or pop stars, even fictional characters. They could also be invited to split the eight cards between people (real or imaginary) that they admire and people they dislike and so on.

The final observation I'd make about triadic elicitation is that, even if the child includes him- or herself in the pool of eight names, this activity tends to reveal – rather obviously perhaps – more about how a child sees others than how they see themselves. That is not necessarily a problem; it depends entirely on what information you are looking for.

Drawing 'Me as I am'

There are a number of reasons why encouraging a child to draw is a good way of supporting construct elicitation and exploration. For younger children particularly, drawing can help articulate things that would have to remain unknown if words alone were wanted. For children and young people of all ages it is sometimes easier to draw than to talk even when one has got the necessary words; embarrassment or awkwardness can be avoided and expression can follow a much slower and more diffused path than conversation partners normally allow. Some children simply struggle to describe themselves or their worries but find no difficulty at all in drawing these things and *then* talking as they draw, or talking about their finished pictures.

Let me say very clearly that I do not value children's drawings only as a means to construct elicitation, but at the same time it is beyond the scope of this book (and my professional experience) to do justice to the richness of discussion that children's artwork can give rise to. Whenever possible, in whatever medium I happen to be working with a child, I like to reveal the constructs amongst all the other highly valuable information I'm being given. Our business at the moment is construct elicitation, and the use of drawings for this purpose will certainly allow us to work in this way with children that we might not otherwise reach.

The simplest use of drawing as a way of achieving this is to ask a child to draw 'Me as I am' – a picture of him- or herself doing something familiar and typical. Ask them to talk about:

> What are doing in the picture? … Where are you? … How do you look, what are you wearing? … Who (if anyone) is in the picture with you? … How do you feel? … What are you thinking about? and so on.

Encourage them to write their responses to these questions around the picture (or write for them if they'd prefer). There will be much to discuss in what the child has produced and amongst their responses will be a selection of emergent poles.

Other pictures, similarly labelled, will add to the 'child's eye' perspective. 'Me as others see me' and 'Me as I'd like to be' are useful additions, with the same prompts from the adult as above, except that in the case of 'Me as others see me' the prompt questions need to be from others' perspectives – 'What do they say about you?' 'What do they think about you?' 'How do they feel about you?' and so on. Bannister and Fransella (1986) include some useful discussion about issues relating to our sense of the ideal and actual self, and readers interested in pursuing approaches to the use of ideal/actual self drawings in PCP work that exploit the medium more thoroughly than the above activities should find Moran (2001) and Ravenette (1999) illuminating and useful.

Exploring constructs

For the purposes of explaining and demonstrating what I feel are some of the most illuminating methods of construct exploration, I'm going to use a fictional case study ahead of the 'real world' ones in the next chapter. That said, the fiction is based firmly on facts and the construct I'm going to start with is one that I have come across a number of times in my work with children and young people:

Intelligent .... Popular

Unfortunately for a great many children, particularly adolescents in secondary schools, this is an all-too-real dilemma: don't appear to be too clever or you won't fit in.

However baleful the influence of this particular construct, before we proceed any further with its analysis I'd like to use it to point out something about constructs in general that I don't feel is often acknowledged: it seems to me that there is an almost poetic compression of language and meaning in these simple dichotomous constructions. To cast intelligence and popularity in opposition to each other is arguably as 'creative' an act as any artfully chosen metaphor or use of simile in a novel or poem. For the person who sees intelligence as incompatible with popularity, the corollaries of being intelligent would be quite different to those anticipated by someone who would put, say, 'thick' in place of 'popular' above. And one would be living in a subtly different world if being an 'intelligent' person were to be construed as in opposition to being 'attractive', 'rich' or 'someone who works hard'. Contrast poles are rarely merely dictionary-definition opposites, because people are too complex and creative in their anticipations of events for that to be so. Of course, such highly personal construing produces results that are as questionable as they are creative (does one really have to choose between intelligence and popularity?), but as Kelly would want to remind us, that's part of the solution not part of the problem!

Laddering and Pyramiding

Once you have at least one construct you are in a position to explore that person's construing further through two complementary techniques called 'Laddering' and 'Pyramiding'. Laddering tends to take you to a person's core beliefs, their values and assumptions about the world. The image of the ladder represents for me one of climbing down into ever more fundamental parts of a person's construct system. Laddering elicits what I always feel to be 'rock bottom' stuff, which puts you in a very good position to reflect on what appears to be underpinning a person's desire to demonstrate a particular quality or to be a certain kind of person. Pyramiding, by contrast, is more practical, behavioural even. It involves asking – taking the Intelligent/Popular construct above as an example – 'How can you tell if a person is intelligent; what do intelligent people do?' (I've found it most useful when working with children to keep to a relatively simple version of Pyramiding. Fully realised, the technique involves treating each response offered as an emergent pole of a new construct. It's the continued exploration of each answer in this way that creates the characteristic pyramid shape on the page.)

To demonstrate the use of these two techniques for construct exploration I'm going to use a fictionalised dialogue between myself, Simon, and 'John', a 12-year-old boy. The dialogue is not intended to be exhaustive, merely illustrative of the two techniques being discussed. As you read it you might feel that there are other things you would want to ask John – and I'd agree – but for now let's concentrate on clear explanation of Laddering and Pyramiding. We'll assume that the Intelligent/Popular construct has already been elicited through conversation with John and use of one of the techniques discussed earlier. The dialogue starts with the important step of establishing which is John's 'preferred pole' in the construct – what would he *like* to be? – and then Laddering that pole through a series of 'Why?' questions.

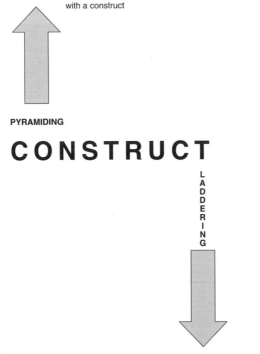

The more practical, 'surface' behaviours associated with a construct

PYRAMIDING

CONSTRUCT

LADDERING

The more 'profound', core beliefs and basic values

Simon:	So John, you've told me that you think of yourself as 'intelligent' and that you would call people who aren't intelligent 'popular'.
John:	Yes, I think so.
Simon:	Which of those two things would you prefer to be, or reckon that it would be best to be?
John:	I'd prefer it if I was popular.
Simon:	Okay, tell me if you can why you feel it would be a good thing to be popular.
John:	If I was popular then people would like me.
Simon:	And why would it be a good thing to have people like you?
John:	If people liked me then I would have some friends.
Simon:	Why would you say that it would be a good thing from your point of view for you to have some friends?
John:	If I had at least one friend then I would have someone to hang around with, someone to talk to.
Simon:	I understand … why would that be important to you, someone to talk to?
John:	When you have a friend to talk to you feel … normal, like everyone else, everyone's got friends.

Let's pause a moment and review what we've learnt from John so far.

+ indicates the pole that John feels describes him best

* is John's preferred pole, what he would like to be

Intelligent+ ……………………….... Popular*

(Why is that important?)

People would like me

(Why is that important?)

I'd have some friends

(Why is that important?)

Someone to talk to

(Why is that important?)

I'd feel normal

Let's resume the dialogue. We'll continue by Laddering the non-preferred pole. Although this is what John does not want to be, Laddering this pole is no less illuminating as it describes how he sees himself currently.

Simon: Let's look at that word 'intelligent', which is what you've called yourself. Now, you've said that you would rather be popular than intelligent so I'm interested to know: what's the problem with being intelligent?

John: If you're intelligent people think you're weird.

Simon: Well I know it might sound like a silly question but why does it matter if people think you're weird?

John: No one wants people to think that they're weird. You get picked on, called names and stuff like that.

Simon: Again, maybe I should know this but what's so bad about being picked on and called names?

John: Every day is like torture. There's not one single minute when you can relax, try to be yourself and just … fit in and get on with what you want to do.

Pause again. Here's what we have now:

+ indicates the pole that John feels describes him best

* is John's preferred pole – what he would like to be

Intelligent+ .... Popular*

(Why does that matter?)

People think you're weird   People would like me

(Why does that matter?)

Get picked on, called names   I'd have some friends

(Why does that matter?)

'Like torture' can't relax or   Someone to talk to

be yourself   I'd feel normal

Let's continue by Pyramiding both the preferred pole and the non-preferred pole. This basically involves asking how you can tell when someone is intelligent, popular or whatever that pole happens to indicate. Unlike Laddering, which takes us to fundamental core beliefs and assumptions, Pyramiding tends to offer up something more like a person's 'working definition' of an attribute or behaviour.

Simon:	John, tell me how you can spot a popular person; what do they do, is there something that really lets others know that they are popular?
John:	Yeah, popular people are always surrounded by other people, they're always talking to someone, people are always listening to them and laughing at their jokes.
Simon:	Are there any other ways in which popular people stand out? If you and I walked through your school now and looked into the classrooms could you pick out the popular people just by the way they look or what they're doing?
John:	Popular people will most probably be smiling a lot, they'll look happy. In class they will be putting their hand up to answer questions.
Simon:	Is it only popular people who put their hands up to answer questions?
John:	Well, not only popular people but you would be more likely to do that if you were popular.
Simon:	Why is that?
John:	Well, you know, if you put your hand up and you're not a popular person straight away someone's going to call out something about you. And if you get the question right someone's definitely going to call you something. I'd rather not bother.
Simon:	Okay … what about 'intelligent'? How can you spot an intelligent person, what do they do?
John:	Intelligent people will probably be sat on their own, or just be on their own wherever they happen to be.
Simon:	Anything else? Are there particular things that intelligent people do?
John:	Yes, they probably won't look at you if you were walking around the school, they would, you know, look at the floor or something in case if they look at you, you might say something to them.
Simon:	Are those the main ways of knowing when someone is intelligent?
John:	They'll also get good marks in tests but they won't tell you about it unless you really make them.

Let's look at the fully Laddered and Pyramided construct:

+ indicates the pole that John feels describes him best

* is John's preferred pole – what he would like to be

Get good marks but won't say	Put their hands up
Won't look at you	Smiling, happy
Sat on their own	Surrounded by others
Intelligent+	**Popular***
People think you're weird	People would like me
Get picked on, called names	I'd have some friends
'like torture' can't relax or be	Someone to talk to
yourself	I'd feel normal

Before we look in more detail at the further possibilities – for John and for Simon – arising from this dialogue, let's pick up what I feel are some important discussion points and one or two caveats as well.

First, you may have asked yourself how I judged when to stop questioning John, particularly when Laddering (Pyramiding in fact is easy in this respect – stop when they have no more to say!). This is certainly a matter for good judgement and there is no hard and fast rule. My experience tells me that three or four 'Why?' questions are usually sufficient to get to a response that feels so fundamental or 'core' to a person's world-view that a further question would be unnecessary, perhaps even insensitive. You can see that I stopped asking John about the advantages of popularity when he said, essentially, that he would feel 'normal' if he were popular. I could have asked: 'Why would it be a good thing to feel normal?' but my judgement was that this question was not needed; I knew enough about John's construing at that point. In fact I myself would struggle to answer a question like that and whilst we have to be careful not to put our thoughts and assumptions into others' mouths that's not a bad rule of thumb to guide your good judgement. A similar thought process led me to stop questioning John when he told me that every day was 'torture' and he couldn't just be himself and fit in.

You will hopefully have noticed also my attempts to make the Laddering 'Why?' questions as conversational as possible. This is vital. If you can't manage this you will sound rather cold and robotic as you simply repeat 'and why is that a good thing? …' over and over again. To get something like realistic answers to those questions you need to be able to pose them in as realistic a manner as possible, a manner that keeps the whole exchange sounding like conversation rather than interrogation (which is an ever-present danger). You can see that when asking John why he feels that something is bad I acknowledge that 'it might sound like a silly question' or 'maybe I should know this'. It's my personal preference to frame such questions in that way, based on an uneasiness with having to ask – as you inevitably will have to – 'what are the bad things about being bullied/hit/picked on/without friends/thick' etc. Take care that asking the question does not hint that you're surprised to hear anybody saying that there are any negative consequences to being in that situation.

It is a fascination of Laddering in particular that one never knows where it will lead and it frequently raises issues that would be impossible to anticipate without this 'climbing down' into the meanings that underpin the construct. From time to time I have seen adult participants in PCP training sessions amaze themselves with the words that come out of their mouths as they allow a colleague to lead them through the process of Laddering one of their constructs. Someone who is highly motivated to be 'successful' at work might find himself saying how important it is to make his dad proud of him. Another person with ostensibly the same construct might be striving to be 'successful' in order to accumulate wealth to guard against an uncertain future. For some, being 'popular' is a way of exerting a positive influence on many lives; for others it is a means of ensuring that one never has a lonely evening. For John in the example above it is a passkey to feeling like a normal human being. You don't know until you ask.

Where next?

So what are the possible next steps or actions in this dialogue with John, given what our exploration of his construct through Laddering and Pyramiding has revealed? There are many possibilities but what there *isn't* is a prescriptive list of things to do next. PCP doesn't claim to help make diagnoses that allow for clear-cut courses of 'treatment'. We would need to know John better than we do at the moment in order to decide where to go next in this situation, and indeed we would need to discuss some of our ideas with him to find out what he felt. However, although John is a fictional character and we can't get to know him better, it would be helpful at least to speculate on further actions, so let's look at some possibilities.

Never underestimate the value of saying to someone 'It seems to me that you're saying/you believe/you think ...' It may not be necessary to try to draw any conclusions or make any inferences from what you have heard, just reflect back what you feel you have heard and ask, John in this case, to comment. He might feel that what you've heard is not what he thought he'd said, or wanted to say, and he might tell you so. There are issues about age and maturity to be taken into account here though. I would have no hesitation in doing that in this scenario in which I have said that John is 12 years of age. If John were eight then I might be a little more cautious. Just because someone has been able to give you a lot of information about himself does not mean that he will be comfortable hearing or reflecting on all of that information at once. Equally, as some of the case studies will show later, it is often quite a challenging message to hear when one's constructs are explored and the results laid out for perusal; you need to make good judgements about whether it is responsible to ask a young person to face that challenge.

The Intelligent/Popular construct could be said to have John trapped. As Kelly put it, he's painted himself into a corner. Apparently, if he's intelligent he can't be popular and so can't have friends. One could challenge John to reconstrue this situation by trying to think of someone who might be intelligent *and* popular. In other words, is there a construct:

Intelligent and popular .... Intelligent and unpopular?

What might 'Intelligent and popular' people do, how might they behave? Is it possible that John could experiment with behaving in any of those ways?

Laddering on both sides of the construct finished with answers from John that could be treated as new emergent poles – 'normal' and 'be yourself'. We could elicit the contrast poles and explore these constructs.

When can John ever manage to 'be yourself'? Does he manage to do this in spite of the perceived disadvantages of being intelligent? How could he be 'himself' more often than he manages now?

Has John ever had a friend? If so, how does this affect the Intelligent/Popular construct, given that John feels that only popular people have friends? Conversely, could John imagine popular people not actually being happy and perhaps even being lonely (plenty of high profile examples amongst film and pop stars)? If so, what else might it be that attracts friends and allows someone to be happy if simply being popular is not enough to achieve that?

Could John experiment with new behaviours to see if they make him more popular? He could try doing some of the things he listed in the Pyramiding of 'popular': if that's what popular people do, could John do some of those things too? Could he try to avoid doing some of the things that 'intelligent' people do?

Salmon Lines

In her book *Psychology for Teachers*, Salmon (1988) describes a method of exploring the sense children make of their own situations using donated constructs that are nevertheless couched in children's own language. The construct becomes a framework within which rating and scaling questions can be used. I'm offering an example below, and in the case studies chapter, of the use of Salmon Lines to help investigate the context of the development of a child's literacy skills. This is the area in my own practice within which I find most use for the technique but readers should easily be able to imagine turning any construct, personal or donated, into a Salmon Line and exploring it in the same way.

Although at first sight the questions below don't appear to be constructs, with only a little mental reorganisation it should be clear that the No/Yes scale is actually a very lightly disguised construct (as are most bipolar rating scales in fact). In the case of the first question, 'Do you like reading?', the donated construct is

Don't like reading .... Like reading

My preferred format for presenting these questions to children and young people is to use an A4-sized laminated card. I make handwritten notes of children's responses on a separate sheet of paper. (If you are not as concerned as I am to have a reusable resource it would also work well to use an unlaminated copy and to write and make marks directly on it.) The card sits on the table between us and makes a useful visual prompt. I explain to children that I want them to answer each of the main questions (which I offer to read aloud if necessary) not in words but by pointing to a place on the line – anywhere they like from *definitely no/not at all/no way* to *definitely yes/yes I am/very much*. As each new question comes up I find it's helpful to restate the No/Yes poles in language that helps the child remember that the line is a continuum. I therefore also take a little time to ensure they understand what the intermediate points on the line might mean:

If you think: 'so-so, maybe, a little bit yes and a little bit no, somewhere in between', then you could point in the middle perhaps. If you think 'yes' but not 'definitely yes' then you might want to point here [indicate roughly three-quarters of the way along the line]. If you think 'no' but not 'definitely no' then you could point here [indicate close to the No end]. It's up to you.

Do you like reading?

NO_____YES

Let's now work through the series of questions about reading.

Do you like reading?

> So, if you really like reading, you think it's great, then point here [indicate Yes]. If you really don't like reading at all you could point here [indicate No] and [etc. for the intermediate points]

Make a note of the point on the line that the child chooses for their answer. These are some possible follow-up questions to ask before moving on:

> Is there a reason why you feel that way?
>
> Have you always liked/disliked/felt like that about reading? [If difference indicated, note point on the line]
>
> What happened to change your mind?

Do you do much reading?

> If you do loads of reading then point here ... if you do no reading at all ... [etc.]

Note the point on the line chosen. Some possible follow-up questions are (as appropriate):

> [If any response other than None] What sorts of things do you read?
> When do you usually do your reading?
> How much reading would you *like* to do? [Indicate the line again]
> [If difference indicated] Why is there a difference ...?
> [If no reading at all] Why is that?

Are you good at reading?

> If you feel you're really good, brilliant at reading … if you think you are no good at all, really bad at reading … [etc.]

Note the point on the line chosen. Follow up as appropriate:

> Have you always been that good/found it that hard/been in the middle?

> [If difference indicated] How did you get from there to where you are now?

> How good at reading do you think you'll be in a year's time?

> [If difference indicated] What is it that will move you from where you are now to there?

> If I asked your teacher/mum/dad/carer/etc. how good you are at reading what would they say?

> [If difference indicated] Why do you think they would say something different to what you've said?

> [If child has indicated they are not a good reader] Think of someone you know who is good at reading. Where would they be on the line? How did they get to be that good?

Do you read in school?

> Do you get a chance to read in school? If you do lots of reading in school you could point here … if you do no reading at all in school … [etc.]

Note the point on the line chosen. Follow up as appropriate:

> [If Yes] When do you read in school?

> How often do you read? For how long?

> Where do you normally read in school?

> Do you read on your own, in groups, or …?

> What sorts of things do you usually read?

> [If No, find out why!]

Do you read at home?

Do you do any reading at home? If you do lots of reading at home …
if you do no reading at all at home … [etc.]

Note the point on the line chosen. Follow up as appropriate:

[If Yes] When do you read at home?

How often do you read?

For how long?

Where do you normally do your reading?

Do you read anywhere else apart from at home (and school)?

What sorts of things do you read?

Do you read to someone or just to yourself?

[If No, explore!] Why not … would you like to … [etc.]

Does someone read aloud to you?

Do you get the chance to just sit back and listen while somebody else
reads to you? If that happens a lot you could point here … if you
never get a chance to do that … [etc.]

Note the point on the line chosen. Follow up as appropriate:

[If Yes] Who reads to you?

When do they read to you?

What sorts of things do they read?

Do you like having someone reading to you?

Would you like to have someone read to you more often? How much
more [indicate the line again]?

What could be done to help that happen?

[If No, explore!] Is there a reason why nobody reads to you?

Would you like someone to read to you?

[If Yes] Who? What would you like them to read? When? How could
that be arranged? [etc.]

4

What use is Personal Construct Psychology? Nine case studies

As yet, few, if any, scales have been developed which tap the child's perception of their own behaviour. Personal construct theory offers the possibility of understanding what sense the child makes of his own actions. (Butler and Green 1998)

In this chapter a range of case studies is offered to give some illustrations of the value of using PCP when working with children and young people. The intention is also to demonstrate 'real world' outcomes of the techniques that were discussed in the previous chapter. I want to emphasise a few points before looking at each case study in detail, principally in the interests of keeping a sense of perspective. Much as I feel passionate about this area of psychology I would be doing more harm than good if I were to give anyone the impression that it is a panacea.

It's sometimes said that 'happy endings' are just stories that haven't finished yet, and whilst I might not agree with the implied pessimism of this view, it does offer a useful warning about presenting too tidy a narrative when describing any kind of intervention into another person's life. All of the situations described in these case studies were complex. Such is life. Although use of PCP often occasioned what we might call 'Aha!' moments for me, the young people I was working with, their families and other adults involved, these moments of insight and re-construing rarely functioned like magic bullets, transforming troubled or unhappy people into relaxed, confident souls through the power of applied psychology. Sometimes the best thing to arise was the asking of a different sort of question about what was going on. Sometimes it was 'merely' that someone felt they understood someone else better, even if the original 'problem' hadn't immediately gone away. So no quick fixes here, but plenty of new possibilities.

I'd also like to put some distance between the work described here and the tenacious myth of the lone hero-innovator professional. I am not attempting to present anything like exemplary casework. In none of these case studies was the use of PCP the only support or influence being brought to bear on the young people involved. What I'm presenting might be better described as snapshots: small sections cut from longer conversations which were in turn only small parts of complex lives. I cannot do justice to that complexity here: there were often other professionals involved with these young people and there were always parents, carers, teachers, friends, peers etc. exerting their influences and playing their parts. Where PCP was effective and useful in these cases it was effective and useful within that larger network of relationships, not in spite of it or alongside it. What I can't do here is give a fair picture of all those other involvements; that would require a different sort of book.

One last caveat: the restrictions of space do not even permit me to report and discuss all the PCP-based work that I carried out with each young person. In most cases only the exploration of a single construct, perhaps two, that seemed to be pivotal or particularly influential in the presenting situation is given here. In each case other constructs were elicited and explored and many other issues were raised in the conversations that took place, often through use of the Let's Talk programme.

Although I wasn't aware of overarching patterns when I was doing this work with children and young people, reflecting much later on the outcomes suggested to me that the very different situations these people were in often had elements in common. These elements seem to me to represent broader dilemmas that I feel we all face from time to time. With this is mind I'm presenting the case studies in groups under three headings that try to capture those human dilemmas: 'Why should I be normal?', 'How can I change?' and 'Appearances are deceptive'. All the case studies have been anonymised. In some cases minor details in the conversations reported have been changed or removed where failure to do so might have made identification of the young person more likely within the local authority where the work took place.

Appearances are deceptive

Work with Annie, Sean and Robbie is described in this section. In each case the theme that seemed to emerge most powerfully was the revealing of another greater and more immediate problem for them than the one that had brought us together in the first place.

Annie
I met Annie three times over a period of 6 months or so. She was a 10-year-old girl described as isolated from her peers and frequently the victim of bullying in

the form of name-calling and deliberate ostracising. Annie was described as having difficulty making and keeping friends and her self-esteem was felt to be low by adults who knew her well. In school Annie was felt to be annoying other children through well-intentioned but socially 'clumsy' attempts at ingratiating herself with them.

Using the triadic elicitation method with Annie revealed that 'geek' was a term she used to describe herself and sometimes others. Treating this as an emergent pole I asked Annie what she would call people who aren't geeks. Her response was 'popular' and she expressed a very strong wish to be a popular person. This was not particularly surprising given the information that I already had about Annie before I met her. Indeed, without ever meeting her I might have guessed that she would wish she were more popular with her peers. Where PCP proved its worth, as it almost always does in such situations, was in allowing me to unpack with Annie exactly what 'popular' (and 'geek') meant to her, or rather, what the corollaries of being popular were for Annie. It's likely that at a superficial level Annie and I both agreed on the dictionary definition of 'popular' but in this context 'popular' had a much more specific and personal meaning for her, and Laddering the construct of which it was one pole was able to reveal this meaning.

Popular*	Geek+
Get attention, don't get called names	Get picked on, jumped on
Lets you know you're loved	Lose your self-confidence
Won't be pushed out of the family	Chicken out of things
	Don't get into things like choir
	Everyone will think she's not good to hang out with; I'll be left with no friends
	It's like my heart is in a locked cell

* where I'd like to be
+ where I am

Looking at the mapped out construct you can see that Annie's sense of being a geek included a very mature analysis of some of the consequences of bullying and social isolation. Sadly, this construct is not without a degree of predictive efficiency. Children *perceived* to be geeks will, whether we like it or not, often not be popular. This is an important point in the rest of the discussion because it means we wouldn't necessarily try to challenge the construct itself, but instead we might try to help Annie to find ways of moving to the 'popular' end.

Annie was articulate and seemed to enjoy being asked to talk about herself. Her deconstruction of 'geek' ended with the unhappy rhetorical flourish that 'my heart is in a locked cell'. At the other end of the construct Annie quite quickly took us from a reasonably easy-to-anticipate advantage of being popular – positive attention – to an expression of the need to feel loved, and from there to a statement about feeling 'pushed out of the family'. Annie did indeed feel that she was somehow not as much a part of her family as her (male) siblings. She based this on her perception of the amount of time her dad spent talking to and listening to her, compared to her brothers. She also felt that she had to initiate in order to receive any signs of physical affection such as hugs from him, again in contrast to her brothers. (It was interesting, but beyond the scope of what I had time to explore, that Annie felt that her mum did pay her the attention and display the genuine affection she felt she deserved. But this seemed to count for little, and indeed appeared to be to some extent cancelled out by dad's behaviour.)

I talked to Annie about what she wanted to happen next. She wished that children in school would stop bullying her and that her dad would spend time with just her, doing simple things such as going out to the shops or sitting together at home and having 'catch-up' time. She agreed that I could talk to her parents about what she had said to me but for various reasons a number of attempts to arrange a meeting with them were unsuccessful. However, when I next met Annie she was far happier, by her own admission (and that of her teacher), than she had been for a long time. Although we had been unable to meet, her dad had read the written report I had sent out following the previous meeting with Annie and had subsequently been spending a lot more time with his daughter, much to her delight. Annie said that her dad had told her he didn't realise she felt left out and was more than happy to do the things she had asked for. Ultimately, within the time that I knew her, Annie's situation in school didn't change greatly but she was nevertheless happier and staff became less concerned. When the circumstances at home changed, her perception of, and responses to, her difficulties at school also changed.

Sean

Sean was a 13-year-old boy whose difficulty was described to me before I met him as mainly to do with relatively poor literacy skills. Coupled with this – caused by it, it was assumed – was Sean's tendency to work very slowly and laboriously in lessons and thereby complete very little of the tasks that were set for him. Sean was perceived to be a boy of at least average ability and there was a general sense that he should certainly be doing more. My work with Sean focused initially on literacy issues but moved very naturally into areas of motivation and self-perception. Sean was 'up front' about his difficulties and admitted that his work rate was slow. We talked for a while about how to improve this situation before Sean described himself to me as 'friendly' and 'lazy'. Eliciting contrast poles and Laddering the results revealed the following.

Friendly*⁺ .... **Bullies**

More friends

Stick up for you when
bullies come

Otherwise you'd just be
beaten up

Get less friends

No help if someone
stronger comes along

Lazy⁺ .... **Hyperactive***

Slower,

Can't run fast

Will get hurt more

Get stronger, fitter

Thicker skin

Can run away if
someone tries to
attack you

* where I'd like to be
+ where I am

This is a good example of an occasion when it felt absolutely right to reflect the
contents of both constructs straight back to Sean. I told him how unexpected it

seemed to hear him refer time and again to aggression directed towards him: whether listing the merits of being friendly or the downsides of being lazy, Sean's thinking was dominated by the desire to escape physical harm – to 'run faster' and develop a 'thicker skin'. We talked about his day-to-day experience of school again in the light of this new information and Sean admitted that he was being bullied on an almost daily basis. Had he tried to involve members of staff? He had once or twice some time ago but had given up because he perceived that he was not being taken very seriously. Sean agreed with me that he would take it upon himself to raise this issue again with his new head of year after our meeting; I would also talk to her to make sure that she understood the impact that bullying was having on him. Our combined effort seemed to be effective, particularly as it was so easy to demonstrate what an oppressive influence his experiences of violence and intimidation were having on his thinking. A subsequent 'catch-up' with Sean's progress revealed that whilst he may have made only modest improvements in his work rate, he felt happier and less intimidated in school.

Robbie

I met Robbie when he was eight years old and in a lot of trouble. Both at school and at home where he lived with his mum and his older brother he was described as disruptive, aggressive and often refusing to comply with requests from adults. In addition, Robbie was felt to have low self-esteem and difficulty making quality friendships with others. I asked Robbie to try the '5 or 6 words that describe you' activity. Amongst the words that he used were 'naughty' and 'friendless'. Further exploration revealed the following:

Safety* .... **Naughty⁺**

Could get seriously hurt   Told off a lot

Everyone would be worried   No friends

People care for you   Lonely

You know some people like you   Feel sad

You could be lonely

I wouldn't like that

Friendless⁺ .... **Nice***

Nothing to do   People like you

Be bored   Never feel lonely

Lonely   Won't be sad

* where I'd like to be

+ where I am

The sadness of Robbie's situation hardly needs interpretation. Look at the way that 'lonely' occurs as a preoccupation for Robbie under all four Laddered poles here, regardless of whether it is the preferred or non-preferred pole that is being explored. Equally, 'safety' is quite an eye-catching term. I think Robbie might have meant to say 'safe' and was perhaps hearing an echo of 'naughty' as he considered its contrast pole. Nevertheless, 'safety' is the word he chose. What Robbie was expressing was a very fundamental need indeed. Readers familiar with Maslow's (1970) hierarchy of needs will recognise 'safety' as second only to the basic physiological needs of food, drink and sleep in terms of its importance to human wellbeing. It wasn't clear why this need was unmet for Robbie until we talked more about home life. Robbie's older brother, Jimmy, was hitting him fairly regularly at home and there was nowhere in the house that Robbie could go where he could feel safe; he had to wait for his brother to go out before he could relax.

The boys' mother thought she knew about her elder son's aggression towards his sibling but she didn't know the extent of it or the effect it was having on Robbie's general sense of wellbeing. Jimmy had his own issues and was well known to a number of support agencies at that time. Support for Robbie at home seemed to need to focus initially on keeping the boys apart – albeit that this was a strategy addressing the 'symptoms' and not the underlying causes of their difficulties. This would at least ensure that Robbie could have some guaranteed and predictable safe space. Fortunately Jimmy enjoyed visiting his Gran, who was within walking distance of the boys' house, and was more than happy to do this if given the opportunity. At school it was possible to facilitate reconstruing of Robbie's aggression somewhat when he was perceived to be so often on the receiving end of aggression himself. Support focused on helping Robbie to recognise and manage his angry feelings (appropriate at school but more problematic at home where Robbie arguably had a legitimate need to be aggressively angry about his treatment) and also on helping to nurture appropriate friendships for Robbie from amongst his peer group in order to help address his sense of loneliness.

Why should I be normal?

These next case studies show three children – Daniel, Chester and Hayley – with what might be called unconventional aspirations or very personal definitions of normal and desirable behaviour. For two of them this gave rise to a degree of conflict with those around them. The difficulty for me in working with these young people was that asking them to change their behaviour would have been very close to asking them to be someone they didn't want to be. These conversations needed more care than most and constraints of time often meant that the best job I could do on their behalf was simply to share their thinking with others and ensure that they were understood if not always approved of. More than any of the other case studies here, the three in this section exemplify for me the notion of children's behaviour being a solution before it becomes a problem. As adults we often don't understand this solution because we don't know what problem the young person is trying to solve.

Daniel

Why was Daniel (aged 12 years) getting into so much trouble at school? His parents were concerned and so were the staff whose lessons he was disrupting. Daniel was often referred to as 'rude' in school and he had received some exclusions for his attitude towards, staff and work. His parents in particular were keen to know what lay behind his behaviour. Could I clarify anything about his motivation that might offer a clue to the best way of helping him change and improve that behaviour?

I found Daniel to be a very articulate young man who was easy to talk to and more than happy to talk about himself. Daniel used the word 'rebellious' to characterise his own behaviour and contrasted this with 'beige' – a wonderfully unexpected term that was synonymous for Daniel with bland and ordinary. Laddering and Pyramiding of this construct revealed the following.

Call out Ask why? Don't always do as they are told	They'd be like the headteacher
Rebellious*+	**Beige**
More interesting, more of an individual	Uninteresting, afraid of a challenge
You've got personality	You won't find out about things
Be recognised for being you	Won't achieve anything, waste your talents
I'd like to be remembered	

* where I'd like to be

+ where I am

It would be hard to overstate the extent to which Daniel saw rebellion as a wholly positive thing. His construct tells its own story. He was dismissive of teachers who were having to put up with his disruption because he felt that the things he was doing (often calling out and interrupting) were legitimate responses to what the teachers were saying and doing. On the other hand, Daniel felt no resentment about being taken to task by teachers or getting into trouble – he seemed to feel that this was the price that had to be paid occasionally, if he wanted to continue behaving in the way he was at that time. Daniel's behaviour seemed to be a very good example of a young person trying to take control of their circumstances in order to validate their sense of who they should be. I talked through issues of responsibility and consequences for him and others; Daniel was ahead of me and had already taken all of this into account. He felt that his behaviour was never going to be so bad that school would exclude him permanently. He was confident that he could control himself well enough to

prevent any very significant disruption to his or anyone else's education. Above all, he identified with what he saw as an unofficial family tradition of standing out and making one's mark on the world. I challenged Daniel to re-think his construct as Rebellious/Calm or Rebellious/Shy – in other words, could the consequences of not being rebellious be positive, or more positive than 'beige' implied? Daniel was not impressed. The alternative to rebellion had to be negative – a necessary distinction, perhaps, in order to justify his behaviour. He talked about both his parents, whom he felt exemplified the rebellious approach in different ways, and other family members who also seemed to fit this pattern. I had to be honest and say that I did not feel there was anything else I could ask or say to Daniel that might cause him to re-think his position.

Although our conversation had been very interesting I was concerned that Daniel's father, whom I met that same day, might expect me to have something more substantial to show for the time spent with his son than a sincere interest in what he had said. To my surprise his father was not only fascinated but also quite moved to hear his son's thinking opened up in this way. He said he felt he had a good relationship with Daniel but had never heard him talk about the issues he had discussed with me. And although he felt that Daniel had somewhat overstated the family's rebellious streak, he could nevertheless appreciate the point his son was trying to make.

To the school staff working with Daniel I suggested that there might be ways of 'calling his bluff' and offering him the kinds of responsibility around school and in lessons that might meet his need to stand out from the crowd without him having to disrupt his own and others' learning. After all, what he actually wanted was to 'be remembered', not to be annoying to others or disruptive *per se*. Daniel's father didn't want any further advice or interpretation of his son's behaviour and had left our meeting apparently quite content. Daniel's profile never rose high enough again for him to be raised with me as a cause of concern.

Chester

I probably shouldn't have shared a 'laugh out loud' moment with Chester when he explained to me the ultimate benefit of being 'skinny', but he caught me off guard. Having called himself chubby and then said he'd prefer it if he was (the contrast pole) skinny, I thought our conversation might begin to digress into issues about body image and anxiety about weight. Chester's construct tells quite a different story.

Chubby build⁺ . . . . **Skinny***

I get some comments from friends

I could run faster

Don't know, it's not too bad actually

I'd be good at games like tag

I'd be able to run away from the police better (but I've only been caught once anyway)

* where I'd like to be
+ where I am

The reason why Chester had caught me with my guard down was because he had pulled off a neat conversational trick and moved a construct that I expected to be somewhere in the self-esteem/self-image part of his system into a discussion about physical performance and running ability. I'm sure he laughed with me because he knew he'd done this too.

For a 13-year-old boy Chester was sadly far too well acquainted with the city's police and youth offending services. His offending mainly involved damage to

property, vandalism and other mostly unplanned and fairly aimless activities that occurred to him and his peers when they were bored. I represented just one of the many other agencies who were also aware of and working with him. I don't believe my work with him made a significant impact on his situation, but with the sheer number of plans wrapped around him that would have been very hard to assess anyway. A difficulty in Chester's situation was that he construed his offending behaviour as an enjoyable pastime, a pleasant way to spend a day in the company of his friends. Exploring the construct above did at least help to clarify the extent to which Chester saw his relationship with authority as a cat-and-mouse game. At the same time he clearly thrived on the esteem he derived from being firmly embedded in a supportive peer group of like-minded teenagers and was very motivated to fit in and impress them. A key focus of subsequent discussions with Chester's mother and other professionals working with him was around trying to engage Chester in constructive activities away from the peer group with whom he was offending and also trying to provide Chester with a mentor in the community who could act as a role model.

Hayley

Hayley was 10 years old when I met her as part of a statutory assessment of her needs. This was a very brief piece of work for me, a single visit to a school that I had not been in before and did not work in again after meeting Hayley. Amongst other issues, Hayley had mild cerebral palsy and was felt to be lacking in confidence. Indeed, Hayley's confidence levels were something of a puzzle. Everyone felt that she could be achieving much more and that it was only a lack of confidence or assertiveness that was holding her back. Hayley's friends often did things for her that she could do perfectly well herself and they were very protective of her in the face of comments from other children about her very slight mobility difficulties. Was there any way that, in amongst the issues my assessment would raise, I could offer advice about helping to improve her confidence?

Hayley did describe herself as 'fretful', explaining that she often felt that things would turn out badly. She wished she could be 'calm', which would make her a happier person she said. I wasn't very surprised to hear her refer to herself as 'disabled', but discovering how comfortable she was with this label was unexpected. Her construct incorporating 'disabled' was interesting to say the least.

Disabled*+ .... People with not as many problems as disabled people

Taken better care of — Will never know what being taken care of that well feels like

Feel safer being disabled

* where I'd like to be
+ where I am

As in the conversation with Chester above, the unexpected quality of Hayley's construct derives from discovering it in a very different place in Hayley's overall system than the position it occupies in mine. Hayley has shuffled a construct that many people would associate with a deficit or a sense of incapacity into a place where it represents 'opportunity' for her. Hayley felt sorry for people who weren't, as she saw it, disabled even though she believed that those people had fewer problems to contend with. For her, being disabled meant being taken good care of and feeling safe – very fundamental stuff indeed that non-disabled people would never experience to the same degree. It seemed that being a 'disabled' person might be for Hayley one way of adapting to life as a 'fretful' person, a reasonably successful experiment to find ways of calling on as much support from others as possible as a buffer against the likelihood that things will turn out badly.

In principle this is a good example of a construct whose overall predictive efficiency is very open to a challenge – is it really the case that you need to be disabled in order to be taken care of? And why did Hayley so often feel that things were going to be bad for her? In reality, time was not on my side and I didn't feel it was appropriate, based on one meeting, to start unpicking a view that Hayley had of herself that helped her to feel secure, albeit that there was a price to be paid in confidence and assertiveness on her part. On this occasion I was able only to represent her views as clearly as possible and to pass responsibility for taking account of and acting on those views to others.

How can I change?

Many children identify themselves as different but definitely do want to change. They have an idea of what constitutes 'normal' or more desirable behaviour and a clear sense of the advantages of behaving or being like that. They can see the benefits of being, as they see it, like everyone else. What they find difficult is taking, or even identifying, some of the steps towards that goal. PCP can be an excellent tool for helping them with this. In this section we'll look at how some of the support for Rory's reading was based on his responses to the use of Salmon Lines about literacy, and we'll also look at Charlie and Toby, whose behaviour was bothering them as much as it was bothering everyone around them. I feel that conversations with children in this situation often have three distinct steps: eliciting the construct poles allows the child to identify him- or herself as needing to change; Laddering both poles reveals why they are unhappy with their current situation and why they think change would be beneficial to them; Pyramiding, particularly of the preferred pole, encourages them to articulate the behaviours that would be needed to bring about the desired change. Pyramiding the preferred pole becomes, in effect, a type of personal target-setting. Let's look at three cases where this approach helped to support children to make their behaviour more congruent with their image of themselves as they wanted to be.

Charlie

I met Charlie at his infant school where he was causing great concern to staff and to his mother at home because of his angry, disruptive and aggressive behaviour. Charlie was seven years old at the time. He described himself as 'not normal' and contrasted this with 'normal'. Charlie expressed a wish to be normal. The Laddering of the construct below shows the great unease that Charlie felt, a considerable burden for someone of his age.

I can't handle myself anywhere	Complete computer games
I can't remember things	
Not normal[+]	**Normal***
Tell lies sometimes	There're loads of normal people and they're better than me
That's not being good	

* where I'd like to be
\+ where I am

Charlie offers a very childlike and personal working definition of what it means to be a normal person – you'd be able to get through to the end of computer games. The Pyramiding of 'not normal' gives some clues as to why Charlie found it so difficult to be this sort of person – with greater insight than you might predict for his age, Charlie portrays himself as essentially out of control and struggling to remember information.

You have to be worried for Charlie when you see him using a construct as fundamental as Not normal/Normal about himself. Such a judgement would be more comfortable if it were occurring in his 'constructs about behaviour', but Charlie's view is not that optimistic; he's talking about the

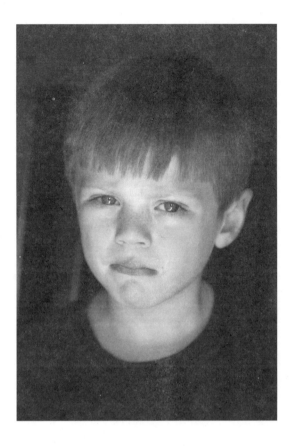

kind of person he is. When very young children use language like this our concern is heightened by the possibility that they are repeating things they have heard said to and about them.

One could set a verbal challenge for Charlie under these circumstances and ask him to reconstrue 'normal' – might it be possible to be 'normal' and yet still not be able to complete computer games? In fact what was wanted here was a more practical, 'acted out' challenge to Charlie's construct and consequent view of himself as out of control and forgetful. Could Charlie be helped to feel more like a normal person by actually managing to concentrate on and complete some games on a computer? This was never going to transform his self-image or behaviour entirely but helping Charlie to access games software that he could complete either with some minimal assistance or alone was one of the strands of support embedded in the wider plans that helped to keep Charlie relatively calm and focused in school.

Toby

One of Toby's constructs turned out to be a particularly good example of the three distinct steps I referred to above. We can see Toby acknowledging a need to change and a desire to be different. For a 13-year-old he had a very firm and realistic grip on the pros and cons of his current situation and with this greater maturity he was better able than Charlie, for example, to evaluate his situation in terms of constructs about behaviour rather than constructs about personality (Toby was at pains to point out that 'Stupid (daft)' and 'Bright' were ways of acting, not labels

about ability). He was getting into a lot of trouble at school for rudeness and disruption, had received a number of short exclusions and was felt to be at risk of permanent exclusion. I've chosen this example in particular because what Toby offered in response to Pyramiding the preferred pole became, with a little further discussion and clarification, part of a new set of targets for him in a revised behaviour plan. Toby had effectively been able to set his own targets in his own language, and all within the context of a discussion about something that *he* wanted to be. This plan, and subsequent reviews and modifications of the plan, was part of a package of support that kept Toby in school and helped to prevent the permanent exclusion that some thought was inevitable.

Giggling	Put their hand up
Do playfighting	Walk, not run
Won't work	'Civilised conversations' in the playground

Stupid (daft)[+] .... **Bright[*]**

Get into trouble	No exclusions
DTs don't help your reputation	No reputation
Get excluded	Don't have to work as hard
	No trouble

* where I'd like to be

+ where I am

Rory

Finally in this 'How can I change?' section we'll look at an example of the use of Salmon Lines as a way of embedding a literacy skills assessment in the broader context of the child's perceptions of their ability, their progress and what we might call the literacy environment around them. I'm not going to discuss all the other work done by me and others with Rory; this is an opportunity simply to show the contribution that PCP made to those other strands of assessment. I was asked to meet with Rory in order to help advise around appropriate support for the development of his reading skills. Rory was nine at the time and despite a range of support in school over a number of years he was still struggling with basic skills of phonological awareness, letter/sound recognition and reading of both high frequency and phonically regular words. As part of my assessment work I asked him a number of questions in Salmon Line format under the broad heading How do you feel about reading?

Do you like reading?

No X_____ **Yes**

The X is Rory's mark on the line to indicate how much he liked reading.

Rory indicated the furthest point on the 'No' end of the line and told me that he had always felt like that. I asked why he disliked reading so much and Rory replied that it was hard and he wasn't very good at it, he couldn't read. Some sensitivity was therefore required with the next two questions (but by no means all struggling readers dislike reading or even identify themselves as having a significant difficulty, the latter sometimes being part of the challenge of helping them).

Do you do much reading?

No _____X_____O_____ **Yes**

The X is Rory's mark to indicate the amount of reading he was doing, the O is his response to the follow-up question of how much reading he'd like to be doing.

Rory said that he sometimes read books in school and also other things on wall displays and the class whiteboard. He explained the difference between his two marks on the line by saying that he wished he could read, he wished it was easy for him so that he could do it more often.

Are you good at reading?

No _O____X__Teacher___N__Mum_____ **Yes**

The X is Rory's own rating of his reading ability. The O is where he felt his reading skills were one year ago, the N where they would be next year. Teacher and Mum are where Rory felt those people would rate his reading skills. (Mum was the parent Rory said would know most about his reading.)

Rory felt that he had managed to move some distance along the line over the last year because he had got older and because he had been receiving help in school.

He expected the same things to continue and therefore he expected his skills to have improved again in one year's time.

Rory felt that his teacher would say he was a better reader than he said he was because 'she knows me'. He assumed (not unreasonably) that his teacher had some kind of 'expert' insight into his reading skills and therefore might know better than he did. On the other hand, he felt that his mum's rating would be too high – unrealistic in other words – because she did not understand about his reading as well as his teacher did, and she heard him read less often. Very rarely in fact.

Do you read in school?

No _____X_____ **Yes**

The X is Rory's estimation of the amount of reading he was doing in school.

Notice that this response appears to be inconsistent with the earlier one in which he indicated that he was doing relatively little reading overall. It probably reflects his sense that reading in school was the greater part of all the reading he was doing. I should also say, though, that using this kind of technique requires a flexible attitude to ideas about consistency – it shouldn't be a problem if two answers don't 'make sense' when laid side by side. That apparent inconsistency could point up a fruitful direction for the conversation to proceed in.

Rory's elaboration on this response indicated that he was mostly reading when the rest of the class or the group he was working in were reading. He had two books at any one time; a 'group' reading book he used when he did shared reading with a lower ability group in class, and – at that particular time – a book about aeroplanes that he had chosen from the school library. He couldn't read the library book, he said, but it was a book on a subject he liked, with good pictures. This was also the kind of thing he wanted to be able to read.

Do you read at home?

No X_____ Yes

The X is Rory's estimation of the amount of reading he was doing at home.

Rory was quite emphatic that he was doing no reading at all at home or anywhere else apart from school. He 'used to' take books home from school to read to his mum but it seemed quite a distant memory for him. He gave the impression now that reading was an activity he associated with 'work' at school and he was therefore grateful to be able to leave it behind when he got home. Would he like to be reading at home again? Yes he would but only if the books were easy. Could anyone help him with reading at home? No, and Rory was at pains to point out how busy his mum and dad were with his younger brothers.

Does someone read aloud to you?

No _____X_____O_____ Yes

The X is Rory's estimation of the amount of time he was able to spend listening to someone else reading to him. The O indicates how much Rory wanted to hear someone reading aloud to him.

'Sometimes' was Rory's initial answer to this question. In fact most of the occasions he could recall of listening to someone else read were when adults at school read instructions out or read aloud from storybooks during literacy work. Rory also mentioned hearing other children read during group reading activities. He didn't find the latter particularly enjoyable but was much more enthusiastic about the idea of having an adult read stories aloud to him more often. At home he knew this could not happen because his parents were busy but he wondered if it were possible in school.

Below are the main issues that were followed up in discussions and acted upon as a result of Rory's reflections during this conversation.

Almost too obvious to need pointing out, but Rory's very strong dislike of reading was clearly doing nothing to enhance his motivation to acquire literacy skills. Either a virtuous or a vicious circle applies in these circumstances – dislike leads to avoidance which leads to stagnation of skills. Or, enjoyment fosters engagement and skill development. Rory's later responses show that he is still 'catchable', still aspiring to be a reader even though he appears unwilling or unable now to take many steps towards that goal. This spark of motivation in the face of years of difficulty is very precious. It's essential in situations such as Rory's to make reading enjoyable and easily accessible in order to keep that motivation alive.

Despite such strong dislike, there is also some small encouragement to be had from Rory not rating himself at the lowest possible level of reading ability. However, we can tell from Rory's descriptions of how his reading has improved and how it will continue to improve that he is making the kind of attributions for success that will not help him to engage more fully with reading and improve. Rory currently sees improvement as beyond his control – it depends on getting help from adults at school and simply growing older. He needs to be helped to see the links between *his* efforts and the gains in his reading skills that he has made and could continue to make in the future.

Rory's confidence in his teacher's opinion is good to see and suggests a positive, trusting relationship ('she knows me'). His teacher suspected this already but appreciated hearing it confirmed from another source. This relationship is a valuable asset when it's necessary to ask him to continue to try hard to acquire skills he has gained only very slowly and partially. By contrast Rory is somewhat dismissive of his mum's view, which says more perhaps about how realistic he is about himself than it does about how he sees her. In the longer term it would be good for Rory to feel that his mum and dad knew more about his progress but an investment of time was required on their part to achieve this.

Rory's answers about reading in school remind us that his motivation remains higher than we might predict. He is still seeking out books that interest him; he just can't read them. School needed to help him to access a wide range of books that he could read easily and they needed to ensure they had accessible versions of the kinds of books he wanted to read.

Rory is not reading outside school, which only reinforces the impression that it's a 'work' task, to be avoided once he has time to himself. Neither is he getting any regular opportunities at home to sit or lie back and have the uncomplicated pleasure of hearing a story read to him. His parents (who did not have literacy difficulties themselves) were sincere in their claims to be busy with work and home life, including care of Rory's two younger brothers, but they were prepared to try out a new routine at home which gave Rory an opportunity to share one of his books with his mum or dad and to have a regular time in the evening before bed when one of them read a story of his choosing to him. The family also joined the local library for the first time as part of their new routine at home.

5

Using the Let's Talk
CD Rom*

When we try to pick out anything by itself, we find it hitched to
everything else in the universe. (Muir 1911)

Background

The background to the development of Let's Talk bears re-telling I think, as
it's a set of circumstances that helps to make the case for the programme's
effectiveness.

Several years ago I attended a training day hosted by the Child Bereavement
Trust. The speaker was Atle Dyregrov from the Centre for Crisis Psychology in
Norway. The content was principally Dyregrov talking, very engagingly, about
his work with children and young people who had experienced trauma.
Amongst the other learning that occurred for me that day was a small
observation that Dyregrov made almost in passing. Talking about therapeutic
work with boys in general, he mentioned that he often found them to be
uncomfortable about having to sit facing an interviewer if the questions involved
discussion of thoughts, feelings and other personal matters. Under those sorts of
circumstances boys, said Dyregrov, would rather sit next to the interviewer,
looking away and making occasional eye contact as it suited them. He light-
heartedly suggested that for a boy being asked to disclose personal information
about himself, looking at a blank wall might be infinitely preferable to having to
meet the gaze of another person!

It occurred to me at the time that this principle could easily be applied to the
children and young people that I met with as part of my work. Although I am
not often discussing trauma I do very often ask children to talk about personal
thoughts and reflections on their own situation. But other than being mindful of

---

*Note: This PowerPoint file is best run on versions of Windows XP and later.

the way in which chairs were positioned, this insight didn't impact much on my day-to-day work until I met a young man called Billy. Billy was a very distressed and confused individual who often behaved in very challenging and worrying ways at school, at home and in the community where he lived. Billy gave the impression that he had a lot to say about the world as he saw it but he wasn't really talking to anyone. I spent an uncomfortable 15 minutes with him in school trying to engage him and hold his attention long enough to build some trust and awareness of who I was and how I might help. Billy wouldn't stay still long enough for any kind of conversation, let alone one that might begin to get some insight into his situation. The longest I was able to stretch his attention span for was a couple of minutes when as a last resort I showed him my electronic diary and its card game of Solitaire.

I had to leave Billy that day having failed completely to engage with him. However, I knew that a very small electronic device had held his attention for a short while so it seemed like a good idea to take a larger and much more versatile one – my laptop computer – when I next saw him. I didn't want to play games with him, though, so the simplest strategy to use in order to combine the possibility for engagement that the computer held with my own need to try to find out a little more about Billy was to put some of the questions I wanted to ask him on the computer and see if that made it more likely that he would answer them. In short, it did. Whereas I'd previously been able to hold his attention only very precariously for two minutes out of 15, when I next met him he sat and looked at the laptop screen with me, answering each question as it came up, for a total of 20 minutes in a row.

Why did the laptop have such a transforming effect on Billy's attention, not only holding it for a significant amount of time but encouraging him to talk about himself in a way that he had previously resisted? Of course 'children love computers', albeit a bit of a wild generalisation, is probably part of the answer. The reasons for this would warrant a chapter to themselves, but Dyregrov's insight about boys also seems to me to be part of the answer. The laptop screen offers a very convenient focus of attention away from the gaze of one's conversation partner – a very convenient 'excuse' for speaker and listener to make little eye contact if that's what suits them. I also think that there is a useful degree of detachment from the questions that can be had when they are presented on a computer screen. If *I* ask Who loves you? this will inevitably feel like a very personal and potentially intrusive question. On the other hand, when the computer 'asks' Who loves you? I think that it must feel a little less like *someone* is trying to pick your brains, even though I'm there encouraging you to give me the answer.

In the three years or so since I had that second meeting with Billy, I have developed and refined Let's Talk to the point where I often use it as the focus of meetings with both boys and girls now, regardless of whether I feel they will be hard to engage – it has turned out to be an excellent stimulus for discussion and a platform for exploration of children's construing of their world. Following a conference presentation in 2005, a number of psychologist colleagues helped to pilot an earlier version of Let's Talk. The feedback about its effectiveness, particularly in helping to begin a relationship with previously hard-to-engage children, was very encouraging. Particularly gratifying was the feedback from some colleagues describing situations virtually identical to Billy's – a child who had resisted talking to everyone had spoken about himself or herself in response to Let's Talk.

Using Let's Talk

Let me emphasise as clearly as I can that Let's Talk is *not* in any way meant to replace the adult in a discussion with a child or young person. Rather, it's intended to supplement the skills and knowledge that an adult brings to a conversation in cases where children might be difficult to engage or might simply find a 1 : 1 verbal 'question and answer' session, however brief, to be hard-going. You might also find, as I do, that it's a useful way of structuring a conversation with a child even when it's not especially challenging to engage them.

Any supplementary or follow-up questions that an adult might want to ask can be woven around Let's Talk. It doesn't pretend to be comprehensive; it's a skeleton! For this reason it doesn't start by asking for the child's name. You will surely have already found out that information by the time you settle down with the computer. The logic of the programme does assume that you're using it at or very near the start of your meeting/conversation with a child, though. However, if you choose to use the programme again with the same child in order to review their progress at a later date, then the temptation to assume that some slides can be skipped altogether the second or third time around should be resisted. It's in the nature of the type of questions asked in Let's Talk that the only one that is certain to receive the same answer over time is the child's date of birth.

Let's Talk is designed to exploit some of the features of PowerPoint that make navigating around the slides feel a little like using the Internet. This was done deliberately as a way of enhancing its accessibility and appeal to children and young people. For example, the cursor sometimes changes shape when you roll it over significant objects and it is possible to reveal new information and jump to linked pages by clicking on different parts of the screen, just as in a website. Naturally, the fact that children are allowed/encouraged to click, scroll and select items themselves also helps to engage them. As with all PowerPoint presentations, the next slide can be brought up in a number of different ways. Left and right arrows on the computer keyboard will advance the presentation in either direction. Hitting the Return or Space Bar keys on the keyboard will also move you on to the next slide. However, to enhance the website feel there is a 'page advance' link in the shape of an arrow in the bottom right corner of each screen and clicking on this will also move things on.

For what it's worth, I've found that asking a child to help me locate a plug socket and set up the computer is a great ice-breaking activity in a first meeting, offering an opportunity to begin building a relationship whilst talking about a neutral and safe topic. To get the best from the programme I suggest it is used under exactly the same kind of comfortable, quiet circumstances in which any potentially very personal conversation might occur. The portability of a laptop computer encourages this – I would not expect a child to engage well with the questions in Let's Talk if the only computer available was in an area where the conversation might be interrupted or overheard. It's not possible to type a child's responses directly into the file as a record of a session with a child but I make handwritten notes as we go along. Some colleagues prefer to print all the slides out onto several sheets of paper in the two-slides-per-page format before the meeting and annotate them with the child's responses. This provides a tangible record of the meeting and one that can be copied and given to the child or young person if that seems appropriate. This would also be an obvious option if no computer were available to use, but that's clearly a poor substitute, missing much of what makes Let's Talk engaging in the first place.

The intention is that once you're up and running, the child or young person does most of the clicking and cursor movement required, with prompts from you where needed. Key words in the titles or questions on each screen are picked out in red throughout.

Age range

Having taken feedback from colleagues, children and young people and having used the programme itself in different versions for a number of years, I've found that I can confidently use Let's Talk with young people ranging in age from seven to 16 years. For a short while I used two versions with slightly different text and graphics, one aimed at 7–11-year-olds and the other at the 12-plus age range. The differences were so subtle they were ultimately unnecessary, which is why a single version of Let's Talk is offered here. The adult needs to adjust the support they offer according to the age, maturity and reading skills of the child that they are working with. I have used Let's Talk with children younger than seven but have often then skipped over some of the questions, or parts of questions. As ever, be guided by what the child is able to do with appropriate assistance from you.

1. Let's Talk

I use the first slide to explain some of the features of the presentation, use of the keyboard buttons and so on. Such is the penetration of ICT into schools and classrooms that I've yet to meet a youngster who has not had some experience of using PowerPoint (or so they tell me), although use of a laptop computer, at the time of writing, remains a welcome novelty for many. I like to emphasise here that I will be asking the child I'm working with to do much of the clicking and selecting that's required throughout the presentation. This is a vital part of securing their interest and engagement. I also establish whether reading will be an issue (I probably already know this anyway but it's good to ask) and whether they want to read each slide themselves or would prefer me to do it for them.

2. Confidential?

A single click on the large red 'button' brings the question up. This is a prompt to the adult to raise and discuss this issue, more than it is a prompt to the child, who of course may have no idea what it means. How this is dealt with is a matter for professional judgement.

3. About you

Fairly obvious, and easy to answer, questions. Even though you are likely to know at least some of this information already, feedback from children when the earliest versions of this programme were being piloted suggested they liked to be asked some basic questions about themselves before being asked about their family. Which leads us on to the next slide …

4. Who lives with you …?

One click on this screen brings all the pictures up. They're just a prompt to think about the question.

5. Your friends

Three separate clicks or key presses are required to bring the questions up.

6/7.   What things are you good at ... do you find hard?

This slide and the next one originally had a list of curriculum subjects as prompts. Children's responses showed clearly that they were mentioning what was on the list as much as, if not more than, things they actually felt they were good at or struggled with. The list was putting words into their mouths so now it's just an open question. Experience also suggests that asking What do you like doing ...? is a useful supplementary question, being subtly different to asking what someone feels they're good at.

8.   About you

Successive clicks bring up the two chunks of text. This is by no means the only point during the Let's Talk conversation at which we are 'doing' PCP; from end to end we are asking a child to tell us how they see themselves and their world. However, this particular slide, being a simplified version of Kelly's self-characterisation activity, does set out to elicit constructs in a more deliberate fashion than many of the others. Each word or description offered is an 'emergent pole' which will reward further discussion and investigation.

To save you having to jump between different sections of the book, here's my 'script' for this screen of Let's Talk, reproduced from the discussion of this eliciting activity in Chapter 3:

> Imagine someone wanted to get to know you really well but they'd never met you before. This person says, 'What's [child's name] like? What kind of personality has s/he got, what kind of character is s/he?' Now, you get to answer those questions, you're the one who decides what this person finds out about you. But the challenge for you is this: you can only pick 5 or 6 words to describe yourself – 5 or 6 different describing words or short phrases to say what you're really like. Try to give them a true picture of the kind of person you are. If you were trying to be really honest about yourself what words would you pick?

Be prepared for children offering only descriptions of their external appearance, e.g. tall, dark hair and so on. Remind them that words about what they're like 'inside' are what's needed. Also, as it says above, short phrases or sentences are very welcome, e.g. 'like having a laugh', 'got loads of friends', 'always mucking about'. Construct poles are by no means limited to single words. If a child remains unable to answer these questions then another of the methods we discussed in Chapter 3 for eliciting constructs can be used.

9.   How do you feel?

It's necessary for the child to make several clicks to complete this screen and fill it with pictures representing a wide variety of moods and expressions of feeling. The screen is complete when the How do you feel? text box appears. I'd encourage you to be creative in the questioning you use in response to this slide. I often ask children if they can see a face, person or character who looks like they themselves 'usually' feel at school, at home, with their friends and so on. Take care not to label the pictures yourself as you talk about them; when a child indicates a picture that expresses their mood then you can ask 'How does that person feel?' without any fear of having put words into their mouths. Many other questions are possible, including scaling questions, and this screen can be used as a platform for a lot of discussion about feelings if that seems appropriate.

10.   Who loves you? Who likes you?

Nothing else is revealed by clicking on this screen. Much to discuss though.

11.   What do you think about school?

Successive clicks reveal the first two bits of text, then the child can click on the number line to give their answer to the question. Click again (away from the number line) for the next question, and again for the last one. You could treat this screen as a Salmon Line and explore further using scaling questions (e.g. What would need to happen to move you along the line and give school a higher mark?); other questions might feel pertinent before moving on.

12.   What could you do?

Two clicks are required to bring the text up. In the midst of many other questions asking what is happening around a child it's important not to overlook asking them what their own contribution might be towards improving their situation.

13.   Help?

Again, clicking brings the text up. The red 'button' signals that the screen is complete. Click on one of the 'buttons' and they get taken to a different slide depending on which one they chose.

14.   What would you like help with?

If they clicked 'Yes' to the 'more help?' question then they are taken here before being taken to the final, 'Any questions?' slide.

15.   Any questions?

If they don't want more help, they are taken straight here, where clicking again brings the text up. This is the final slide and it ends with thanks and acknowledgement of the considerable amount of information that the questions will have elicited.

Let's Talk

Developed by
Simon Burnham
A Lucky Duck Resource
© Burnham 2007

www.luckyduck.co.uk   Simon Burnham

Let's Talk

1

Before we start

CONFIDENTIAL?

2

About you

Your date of birth?

Your age?

Things you like to do in the evenings, weekends and holidays?

3

Who lives with you at home?

4

Your friends ?

Who are your friends?

When do you see your friends?

What sorts of things do you like to do with your friends?

5

What things are you good at in school?

Click here

6

What things do you find hard at school?

Click here

7

About you

How would you describe yourself to someone who'd never met you but wanted to know what you're really like?

Try doing it using only 5 or 6 words.

Click here

8

Click here

9

Who loves you?
Who likes you?

Click here

10

What do you think about school?

If you had to give school a mark out of 10, what would it be?

0/10 would mean you feel awful, and 10/10 would mean you feel really good about it.

0 1 2 3 4 5 6 7 8 9 10

Have you ever felt better than that?
Have you ever felt worse?

11

82

What could you do...

To make things better for you
at school?

HOW WILL YOU DO IT?

12

HELP?!

Do you get any extra help with anything at school?

Would you like more help with anything?

Yes
Please!

No
Thanks!

Click here

13

What would you like help with?

Click here

14

Any questions?

Is there anything you'd like to ask now,
or anything else I should know?
Thanks very much for all that information!

Click here to finish

Click here

15

This resource is sold with and forms an
integral element of the publication

Let's Talk

Using Personal Construct Psychology
to Support Children and Young People

Click here

www.luckyduck.co.uk   Simon Burnham

83

References

Bannister, D. and Fransella, F. (1986) *Inquiring Man: The Psychology of Personal Constructs*. Routledge: London.

Burr, V. and Butt, T. (1992) *Invitation to Personal Construct Psychology*. Whurr: London.

Butler, R. and Green, D. (1998) *The Child Within: The Exploration of Personal Construct Theory with Young People*. Butterworth Heinemann: Oxford.

DfES (2001) *Special Educational Needs Code of Practice*. Department for Education and Skills: London.

Fransella, F. and Dalton, P. (1990) *Personal Construct Counselling in Action*. Sage: London.

Kelly, G.A. (1955) *The Psychology of Personal Constructs*, Vols 1 & 2. W.W. Norton: New York.

Maher, B. (ed.) (1969) *Clinical Psychology and Personality: The Selected Papers of George Kelly*. John Wiley and Sons: London.

Maslow, A.H. (1970) *Motivation and Personality*. Harper and Row: London.

Moran, H. (2001) Who do you think you are? Drawing the Ideal Self: a technique to explore a child's sense of self. *Clinical Child Psychology and Psychiatry* 6 (4): 599–604.

Muir, J. (1911) My First Summer in the Sierra. Available at http://www.yosemite.ca.us/ john_muir_writings/my_first_summer_in_the_sierra/chapter_6.html.

Ravenette, T. (1999) *Personal Construct Theory in Educational Psychology: A Practitioner's View*. Whurr: London.

Salmon, P. (1988) *Psychology for Teachers: An Alternative Approach*. Hutchinson: London.

Salmon, P. (1995) *Psychology in the Classroom: Reconstructing Teachers and Learners*. Cassell: London.

UNICEF (1990) United Nations Convention on the Rights of the Child. Available at http://www.ohchr.org/english/law/pdf/crc.pdf.